Towards the Development of Social Capital

Veredigno Atienza

Other books by Veredigno Atienza:

1. Creating Systems of Justice: Philanthropy at the Highest Level
2. Reflections in the Marketplace
3. Primo de Leon in His Prime
4. Passing Thru: a Composite Story
5. In Search of a National Consensus

Philippine copyright 2007
Registration number: A 2007-1325
ISBN: 978-0-6151-6030-6
Published in the USA by Lulu
First Edition
Suggested retail price: USD 12.95
Sales proceeds for the benefit of BSLBA outreach

Table of Contents

This book is dedicated to
Aurelio Sangalang Atienza,
former mayor of Lemery, Batangas; fourteenth person
to be admitted to the Roll of Attorneys of the Supreme
Court of the Philippines; admitted to the Philippine Bar
on October 18, 1919.

Foreword

In its charter year 2005-2006, Barangay San Lorenzo Business Association (BSLBA) launched a quarterly community newspaper named "Linkages". The barangay is the smallest unit of government in the Philippines. Barangays make up towns and cities, which in turn make up provinces. Provinces are coordinated as regions, and in 2006, the country was organized into mega-regions.

In BSLBA's second year 2006-2007, BSLBA converted the newspaper into a magazine. Over the past two years, "Linkages" has generated various articles and contributions which reflect the thinking of various sectors and parties in Barangay San Lorenzo, which together with Barangay Bel-Air, serves as the financial and business capital of the Philippines. BSL and BBA are local units within the City of Makati, the premiere city in the Philippines. (Note: the City of Manila and Quezon City also claim to be the premiere city of the Philippines.)

This book provides a framework for the integration of a good number of "Linkages" articles plus some other related articles or materials. These articles reflect and promote different aspects of Barangay San Lorenzo. They are just a snapshot. They are not comprehensive. What is important is that they were written and contributed in the first place, proof that there are people in BSL who wish to reach out to others within and beyond BSL. These articles are intimations, if not outright proof of the existence of social capital in BSL. They also serve as instruments for further developing social capital.

Capital is necessary for the growth and development of every country. Capital can be in the form of land, location, natural resources, financial capital, intellectual capital, human capital, and social capital.

The value of social capital cannot be underestimated. There are countries in the world with vast acreage, natural resources, even many graduates from top American and European universities, and yet a great amount of its population is poor, malnourished, and living in squalid conditions. Where lies the problem? Most likely, there is a shortage of social capital.

Over the past two years, "Linkages" the newspaper and the magazine has done its share in the development of social capital in Barangay San Lorenzo, a vital locality of the Philippines.

The book concept, structure, editing, layout, and proofreading were done by the undersigned. The sales proceeds of this book are intended for the social outreach projects of BSLBA.

Veredigno Atienza
BSLBA President (2006-2008)

SECTION ONE: INTRODUCTION TO SOCIAL CAPITAL

Social capital is an old notion, and yet in this time and age, it is still hard to pin down. It comes with being human, and yet it is not limited to human beings; the animal world has its own version of social capital. It is an asset, and yet it can also be a liability.

As capital, social capital is an asset on which some return can be expected. Capital can pertain to human beings or to inanimate objects. When it pertains to people, it can be human capital as well as social capital. When it pertains to inanimate matters, it can be financial assets or nonfinancial assets.

Human capital consists of assets peculiar to the individual, such as his level of intelligence, health, education, skills, talents, looks, emotional maturity, and charisma.

Social capital refers to relationships as an asset, covering both the extent and quality of relationships. Social capital refers to connectedness, to bondedness, to relatedness. It refers to being part of a larger whole, ie a small clique as well as a vast network, or even to a constellation of networks. Most important, it refers to the level of mutual trust, and the spirit of teamwork, cooperation, and reciprocity.

US foreign aid offers a powerful experiment in social-political-and-economic behavior. The history of US foreign aid indicates trillions of dollars having been expended to assist other nations. And yet the beneficial impact on the recipient countries shows great divergence. Some countries truly and quickly benefited from aid, others did not.

The following historical phenomena heighten the point above. Examples: the rebound of Germany and Japan after World War Two, the growth of South Korea after the Korean War, the development of Taiwan after the Communist takeover of China.

External aid has had varying effects on recipient nations due to the differences in social capital of recipient nations. Social capital can be considered a critical factor, if not the critical factor, in the differing impact of external aid on the performance of nations

On the whole, social capital can be considered to be a significant predictor of economic performance. The greater the social capital in a country, there is a greater likelihood of economic advancement in that country. Social capital is a predictor of positive performance, of growth and development, of transformation and the full attainment of national potential.

Filipinos are well known to be a charming, hospitable, socialized and sociable people. Filipinos are joiners. They join associations. They network. They join constellations of networks. They love to socialize, and when possible, to party. They stay connected, wherever they may be. On a prima facie basis, Filipinos have a high level of social capital.

Social capital can be a tricky phenomenon. Social capital is based on personal bonds. The bonds are in turn based on personal values. If the dominant personal values are for personal enrichment and glorification and/or for family security and family status, then all other higher and broader values will be in second place if confronted with the above personal values. In such situations, the value of social capital turns from positive to negative. Social capital morphs from asset to liability.

Genuine social capital goes beyond partying, bonding, networking and politicking. There is a need for discernment. There may be a need for changes in the value system, in the definition of self, in the basis of valuation of others, in the basis of social stratification.

The ultimate test of social capital is whether it is based on matters that unite rather than divide. The ability to pull in the crowds is useless, when the ultimate objective is questionable, when it is for a selfish reason, not for a broader and higher interest. The ultimate test of social capital is its quality and the quality of the leadership using that social capital. True and genuine social capital is about service to others, the common good, the general welfare, and the uplifting of the common people to a higher level of material and spiritual development.

There are factors that perennially gnaw at social capital: social competition or the competition for status, political competition or the competition for power, financial competition or the competition for wealth. The perennial enemy of social capital is individual ambition, many times sublimated as family ambition, which is equally toxic and corrosive. The number of ways by which human nature feeds the ego is simply amazing, each way a potential threat to social capital.

Social capital thrives where there is communitarianism, where there is an identification of self with the community and the larger community ie the national community and the international community – in thought, word and deed. Easily the bane of social capital is vested interest and the eloquentia that is bought and paid for by vested-interest groups.

Individual and institutional behavior can promote or detract from social capital. Social capital in turn affects the behavior of individuals and institutions. With discernment, institutions such as barangay associations eg BSL and BSLBA, and community publications eg "Linkages", promote the development of social capital, while drawing on the same social capital for their own growth and development.

The following articles help depict the effort to build up at the community level, the social capital so vital to the development and well-being of both community and nation.

SECTION TWO: BARANGAY SAN LORENZO

Founding of BSLBA

Ernesto Moya
Secretary, Barangay San Lorenzo
Co-founder, Barangay San Lorenzo Business
Association

A City Hall memorandum dated October 25, 2004 enjoined all Makati barangays to organize their respective barangay business associations (bba), in line with the city government's desire to stimulate and promote business within each barangay.

The objectives are as follows: 1) to encourage the entrepreneurial spirit among constituents; 2) to facilitate the exchange of ideas and entrepreneurial know-how among members; 3) to provide a forum for dialogue between private and public sectors on issues affecting the business environment; and 4) to eventually uplift the economic status of the barangay community.

Basic guidelines included organizing a group of convenors who will elect among themselves a Board composed of six (6) barangay businessmen. The seventh will be the barangay captain or kagawad who will be designated as an ex-officio member.

In order to fast track the process, Barangay Chairman Joshua John C. Santiago commissioned Barangay Secretary Ernie Moya to do the organizing. Hence, Barangay San Lorenzo Business Association (BSLBA) was organized, incorporated and registered with the Securities and Exchange Commission on December 29, 2004.

The incorporators were: Ernesto Moya, Jesse LaO',
Veredigno Atienza, Severo Santillana Jr, and Kagawad
Diva Abad Santos.

Mr. Moya assumed the Association chairmanship and
initiated a membership drive among barangay
businessmen. By the end of January, 2005, 190
businesses had joined the Association. As of March 31,
2005, the membership roster had increased to 195, and
the Association had become a going concern.

As the Association was envisioned to be a private
undertaking, there was a need to relinquish the
Association leadership in favor of a private
entrepreneur/member. On April 4, 2005, the BSLBA
Board chose Ms. Ana Maria C. Tanchanco, president
of Taters Enterprises, as the new Chairman. Mr. Moya
was retained as an ex-officio member of the Board.

Message from the Chairman

Joshua John "Jay" Santiago
Chair, Barangay San Lorenzo
Founder, Barangay San Lorenzo Business Association

Barangay San Lorenzo is very fortunate to be home to a multitude of business establishments, ranging from giant corporations to small proprietorships. That the core of Makati CBD is located inside the Barangay is living proof of BSL's prominence as a business mecca.

This year, more than 8000 businesses entities representing various industry sectors registered with our Barangay. This represents a 30% increase over last year's figure. Hence, a sizeable chunk of our Barangay revenues comes from commercial real estate taxes and business-related permits and clearances.

In the face of an ever changing business climate, maintaining our competitive edge will always be a continuing challenge to the Barangay leadership. One thrust therefore of our Barangay Development Plan is to effectively tackle the main challenge of promoting and ensuring an environment conductive to business retention and expansion.

With the creation of Barangay San Lorenzo Business Association, facing up to our challenge will be a task made easier. The much-needed linkage between the Barangay and the business sector is established.

As a forum for the exchange of ideas and as a partnership in common endeavors, this linkage will produce a synergy resulting in a healthier and friendlier business environment.

Editor's Desk

Veredigno Atienza

Most of us did not know each other before, but now we are a great team. I am referring to the board of directors of the Barangay San Lorenzo Business Association.

I am not exactly aware who brought in whom, but I have some idea. Barangay Secretary Ernie Moya invited me. Marlene Po brought in (perhaps shanghaied) Annie Tanchanco. Barangay Captain Jay Santiago and Kagawad Diva Abad-Santos were present from the conceptualization stage. Jesse LaO, Jun Santillana, and Ernie Moya came together as a package. Annie tapped Kuku Lopez. Jesse saw the potential of his anchor tenant Liza Guillermo.

It is a balanced team: male and female, executives and self-employed, SLV residents and commercial building locators, practitioners and academics, rentiers and entrepreneurs, politically active and politically passive. It has a healthy dose of IQ, EQ, and AQ (adversity quotient, the ability to handle adversity, contradiction and challenges).

BSLBA has launched two major initiatives: the BSLBA Business Forum and the "Linkages" newspaper.

The Business Forum hopes to develop a reputation for inviting speakers who can inform, enlighten, and inspire. For the very first Business Forum, we have invited BIR Commissioner Jojo Bunag, who is well-known for his legal expertise and amiability. He has a tough job in his hands, and we wish him well. .

"Linkages" is envisioned to serve as a channel of communication within the Barangay community, and between the community and its larger environment. Just like the Business Forum, "Linkages" is meant to inform, enlighten, and inspire.

Thru "Linkages", we hope that you get to know your community more. You will be pleasantly surprised. Makati is simply great for working, living, and raising children in.

We hope "Linkages" gets your attention, respect, and support. And may each issue brighten up your day.

This "Linkages" issue is a labor of love of the BSLBA board. Every board member contributed to this issue. Thru "Linkages", we hope that people will discover BSLBA and decide to join and be active. We look forward to the day when the by-lines will be less of ours, and more of personalities from the Barangay San Lorenzo community at large: Legazpi Village, Ayala Center, San Lorenzo Village, Pasay Road, Makati Cinema Square, Pasong Tamo, and Ecology Village.

This issue is the maiden issue, and may it speak well for itself.

BSL: Fusing Diverse Commercial Elements with Grace and Style

Bob Chan

Barangay San Lorenzo the local government unit that has jurisdiction over the western half of the Makati Central Business District enjoys many distinctions.

Its nucleus is San Lorenzo Village. Just across this subdivision of over 700 upscale households sprawls the Ayala Center, a 38-hectare mixed-use development with over 500 dining, retail and entertainment outlets.

At the Ayala Center, there are 11 cinemas (make that an even dozen with My Cinema, a 50-seater theater for private screenings); On Stage, a live performance venue which is now home to the PETA; Art Film, a theater dedicated to indie and "non-commercial" films; the Expo Exchange, an exhibition center and trade hall; a chapel; and a three-hectare park that has become a favored watering hole of local society's gliterrati as well as of the Makati financial district's reigning moguls.

Culture and the arts thrive in the vibrant environment of Barangay San Lorenzo, home to the Ayala Museum (with its renowned dioramas depicting important milestones in Philippine history, and its rich collection of Filipiniana), and three art galleries: Galleria Aurora at the village proper, the Luz Gallery at the Locsin Building and the Osmundo Gallery at Dusit Hotel Nikko.

Five of Makati's five-star hotels are within BSL boundaries: The New World Renaissance, Makati Shangrila, Dusit Hotel Nikko, The Intercontinental, and Oakwood Premiere. As are three highly-respected educational institutions: Assumption College, Don Bosco Technical Institute, and the Asian Institute of Management.

At Barangay San Lorenzo's northern fringes are the Makati Medical Center, the Makati Cinema Square, which anchors a chain of shops and entertainment outlets, and a creek-side strip called the Mile-Long Strip.

Even deprived of all these rich features, Barangay San Lorenzo will still have the singular distinction of being host to half of the Makati Central Business District (Legaspi Village) with its hundreds of corporate headquarters, banks, financial institutions, embassies and consulates, and the lion's share of the district's day-time transient population of over half a million workers and visitors.

No other place in the entire Philippine archipelago is able to accommodate and harmonize so many diverse elements. At Barangay San Lorenzo, this magic is achieved with grace and style.

Spreading Our Wings

Veredigno Atienza

We would like to thank everybody who attended the launch of "Linkages" last September 1, 2005 at the Hotel Intercontinental Manila. Since then, 28 new members have joined BSLBA. We would like to believe that the launch and widespread distribution of the maiden issue of "Linkages" have helped recruit the new members.

Charter Chair/President Annie Tanchanco quickly followed up the Intercon affair with an invitation to our over 200 members to join the different working committees of BSLBA. We would like to thank the following BSLBA members who enthusiastically volunteered to join.

Venu Kotamraju of Ace Foods, Inc. and Ellen de Castro of Ball Park Snacks graciously volunteered for the Social Development and Outreach Committee, while the International Exchange Bank volunteered for the Education and Training Committee.

Furthermore, JP Tanchanco of Chimara Café, and Quasha Law represented by Atty. Anna de Vera, volunteered for the Marketing and Promotions Committee.

Congratulations and a warm welcome to you.

Our readers will notice a new feature of "Linkages", namely the Members' Voice Section where we are tapping into the wealth of information and wisdom of our members who have something meaningful to say, but are not inclined to write long articles.

We are grateful to and appreciate the comments of the following contributors: Marjorie Chingbingyong-Lee of Fruitiocca!By Health Gourmet, Jaime Garchitorena of Edupro, Manuel Igual of Cocopalm, Joby Martinez of Urban Effects, Melotte Mondelo of Dusit Hotel, Richard Sanz of Tea Square Food and Beverage, and Noemi Narvaez of Robinson's Savings Bank.

As part of the effort to strengthen the publication, the Linkages Committee has acquired the services of media specialist Bernard Supetran as Editor-in-chief. The Committee will maintain an editorial and oversight function on the various aspects of the publication. A newly-appointed distribution agent will ensure our compliance with our commitment to our advertisers to reach at least 10,000 readers per issue.

In an effort to draw broader participation from existing and potential members, BSLBA will hold its Annual Assembly and General Elections on March 30, 2006. The members will have 10 directors, three being ex-officio directors from Barangay San Lorenzo, while seven will be elected at large. Of the seven, three directors will have a one-year term and four directors will have a two-year term to ensure continuity.

In our first year as a barangay business association, we have become aware of the vast opportunities for social and community service. For example, the Education and Training Committee has lined up various seminars to enhance the skills of its constituency, such as computer literacy, food safety, customer service, supervisory skills, total quality management, secretarial services, etc.

After all is said and done, one thing is getting clearer and clearer: that BSLBA offers an excellent venue for service, and whoever gets actively involved will reap the fruits of reaching out and creating a difference.

So join na kayo.

May peace, prosperity and love be with all our members and readers during the Christmas Season and the New Year.

The Making of a Great City

Joshua John C. Santiago

Bob Talbert once said that "A great city is one that handles its garbage and art equally well." I am proud to say that there is one great city that does just that, and at its forefront is this equally great barangay! Makati is that city and that barangay is San Lorenzo.

Distinguished guests and friends, ladies and gentlemen, I welcome you to Bgy. San Lorenzo. Home to more than 8,000 business establishments, premier education centers, a hospital that is considered an institution, top ranking hotels, various entertainment spots and three booming villages- Ecology, Legaspi and San Lorenzo

My friends, a pleasant afternoon to you all. Indulge me by allowing me to exalt our beloved barangay.

Barangay San Lorenzo has been known to be part of the top financial district of the country. However, we are a mixture of diverse sectors and sad to say, behind this overwhelming financial success lies a community that is depressed, prejudiced against and very much in need of attention. It breaks my heart to see the great disparity between the skyscrapers and the shanties.

On the other hand, I feel blessed to have been given the opportunity to help uplift the living conditions of its dwellers. The task is daunting, but achievable. I am challenged, for I believe that every private citizen has a public responsibility, and every public official an even bigger public responsibility

We have created livelihood programs for our less fortunate brothers; such as candle making, soap making, curtain and bed sheet making, meat processing and a lot more. And the barangay will fund their start - up investments. The candles made by them are being bought by Don Bosco Church located in our barangay, and the soaps are currently being marketed. All these undergo strict quality control.

My dear friends, we are indeed moving not just towards sustainability, but towards a higher level: a symbiotic relationship. We have thousands of establishments. Let us actively involve ourselves and our businesses not only in the livelihood of our brothers but in their lives as well.

Friends, have you come across the Broken Windows Theory? It refers to the reaction of people when they see a broken window, a seemingly negligible part of any infrastructure. A broken window signifies ugliness, neglect, a question of safety. People therefore shy away. Business keeps out. Therefore, if something is broken, we should fix it. I am calling for enhancing our infrastructure and environment to make them more comfortable and more comforting to both investors and customers.

We would also like to give our residents and thousands of transients the opportunity to ENJOY our beloved community. In line with this, we will enhance our parks for we believe in quality family time and the promotion of good health. Our children should be able to laugh and play while breathing fresh air.

But let us not focus on the physical aspect alone. One important consideration is the security of the community: peace and order. We have created Task Force Disiplina, which will ensure that the City and Barangay ordinances are fully implemented. We serve as a check to erring pedestrians, motorists, traffic enforcers, officers and the like. But we do not just apprehend and punish them. We re-educate them..

All these we do to bring about better business. To stay at the forefront of the financial district, we will create satellite business districts to spur the growth of underdeveloped areas, clusters, nooks and crannies in the barangay, while serving the developed business sector even better.

With the management of peace and order, the installation and maintenance of the proper infrastructure, and the organization of the business association, we will move forward to the execution of San Lorenzo's grand master plan.

I call on you, the core of the business sector. Be not reticent; speak out. Be not passive; be doers. Let us all work with zeal towards the dawning of a new era, a new barangay, and a better Makati.

San Lo Forging Ahead

Wivina Ferrer

Chairman Joshua John Santiago's vision for BSL is to be a Singapore: He stressed two of the basic prerequisites that need to be present: discipline and cleanliness. With these, one can achieve peace and order, security and harmony, and a healthy business atmosphere.

Considering that BSL is indeed the richest barangay in Makati, being the home to 8,000 business establishments, the possibilities are endless. The youthful BSL Chairman related his plans and projects, but added that his experience at the helm has taught him to do things a step at a time. He may have drawn up his plans but circumstances are such that it is best to aim for the achievement of one project at a time.

When questioned on projects he has lined up, he enumerated eight different projects, with Task Force Disciplina at the forefront, which will tackle the following: road safety, traffic enforcement, and road signage. He further explained that for a true business atmosphere to prosper, one should put in the proper structure, and ensure that the environment is appropriate for such structure.

Beautification projects also rank high on the priority list. The first is the rebuilding of San Lorenzo Park, the upgrading of the Amorsolo sidewalk, and the beautification of the sidewalk and side area of Ecology Village.

The Building Emergency Procedure, which was first installed in BSL in cooperation with Philvocs is a must for every building.

Inspection of all business establishments is another project BSL Chairman Santiago underscores in terms of priority. He argues that all the businesses that get clearances from the barangay must follow certain standards and criteria. Therefore, it is incumbent upon the barangay to make sure that these barangay criteria are met. Rather than being a duplication of City Hall's work, BSL inspection complements the work of City Hall.

Another big plan is the transfer of the Barangay Hall from San Lorenzo Village to Legazpi Village making the Barangay Hall more accessible to business, which makes up the majority of the membership. The misconception is that Barangay San Lorenzo covers only San Lorenzo Village. However, in truth, Barangay San Lorenzo's borders include Buendia (Sen. Gil Puyat Ave), Pasong Tamo (Chino Roces Ave), Ayala Avenue, and EDSA. Pasay Road (now Arnaiz Road), Paseo de Roxas and Makati Avenue cut thru the middle of the barangay.

The security force of BSL will be increased to thirty personnel. BSL Chairman Santiago said that he has been in close coordination with MACEA and he is giving them ten additional security personnel for patrolling Legazpi Village. Security has a top priority in Santiago's list.

Another notable project is the reclaiming of Pasay Road. Santiago mentioned that research has been conducted and that he has been holding consultations with business owners for this. He wants to build a side walk for Pasay Road, to replace the unsightly overhead electrical wires and cables with underground wiring, and to plant trees. He envisions sidewalk cafes. Although businesses concerned may lose their four-car parking facility in front of their buildings, foot traffic will increase and more business will be created. He promised to allow street parking after 6 p.m.

Santiago talked about maximizing the use of resources which abound in BSL and pointed out that he is planning more college scholarship grants to the children of Botanical area which is the indigent area within BSL. He also talked about his plans to try to employ more of these persons within the barangay to help uplift their lives. In addition, he has lined up more training and seminars to benefit all the members of the BSL.

Chairman Santiago underscored the need for transparency in all plans, projects and implementation. He vowed a barangay that is insulated from political intervention, a barangay that will have a healthy business atmosphere, a barangay that is secure, rally-free, disciplined and a hub for success. He knows this is asking too much of himself, but the Chairman is not just a doer, but also a dreamer. Aren't all young people dreamers?

Reaching Out

Joshua John Santiago

"Linkages" is now Barangay San Lorenzo's official quarterly newspaper, intended as a communication tool designed to link all our community sectors. It shall be owned by BSL, with BSLBA retaining management and operational control. First of all, I would like to thank all sector representatives for the outpouring of articles and materials thereby enabling us to attain a diverse coverage of community issues and events.

With this issue, our editorial team suitably adopted the theme "reaching out". What comes to mind is an extended arm in the act of offering help or assistance. In the process of reaching out to our constituents, BSL's Sangguniang Barangay has come up with plans, programs and projects we deem beneficial and essential based on our assessment of community needs. This however is a role we are duty-bound to perform as public servants anyway.

What I wish to discuss and highlight is the other part of reaching out...another extended arm reaching out. I refer here to our Barangay Volunteers, men and women from the private sector who contribute their time and services in fulfilling specific community needs.

During my term, I am extremely grateful that the spirit of volunteerism is alive and robust. A cordial and collaborative relationship exists between our Barangay and our territorial associations. For this I thank their respective officers led by Atty. Val del Rosario (San

Lorenzo Village Association), Mr. Adolfo Duarte (Makati Commercial Estates Association), Col. Wenceslao Cruz (Ayala Center Association), Mr. Mauricio Martelino (Ecology Village I Homeowners Association), Mr. Severo Santillana (Ecology Village III Homeowners Association), and Mr. Deogracias San Miguel (Makati Parking Authority).

Under the able leadership of Mrs. Rose Sibug on her second term as president, our BSL Senior Citizen Council is as cohesive and vigilant as ever in promoting the welfare and healthy lifestyle of our senior citizens.

With Fr. Bong Javines as executive director and the able assistance of Bro. Tony Caspellan, Don Bosco Pugad continues to rescue street children from the dangerous streets and transport them to a safe shelter for caring, healing and character building.

We also witnessed the birth of three new NGOs now serving as our new partners in participatory governance. These are San Lorenzo Urban Poor Association (SALUPA), Barangay San Lorenzo Business Association (BSLBA) and Persons with Disability & Company (PERDISCO). We owe these to individuals who zealously responded to the calling of community service.

Armed with a desire to uplift the image of Botanical Gardens and to promote self-reliance among its community members, Ms. Rose Malano, now our Barangay Treasurer, mobilized her friends and neighbours to form SALUPA. To date, this NGO has implemented a number of livelihood projects and formed a team of civilian marshals who assist our

Tanods in overseeing peace and order and cleanliness in the area. With these self-policing efforts, we now have a much cleaner and more progressive Botanical Gardens community.

Ms. Annie Tanchanco's dynamism and avant-garde style of executing ideas coupled with Mr. Bernie Atienza's proven organizational expertise account for BSLBA's status as a benchmark business association thereby setting a standard for other barangays to emulate.

A group of parents has a clear and vivid understanding of the need of their physically challenged children to be empowered as active and useful members of our community. They passionately advocated the formation of a support group. As we recognize the noble intent of this advocacy, our Barangay Council supported the creation of PERDISCO, which is now actively headed by Ms. Elizabeth Ona as President and Ms. Dorothy Pasia as Vice-President.

It is but fitting to acknowledge the time and effort expended by Ms. Marlene Po, Ms. Carmina Ortega and Mr. Johanne Quisumbing in co-organizing our Sunday Community Market at Legazpi Park. Same goes to the current working committee composed of vendors who are genuinely determined to work for the market's longevity and success.

Our "Salu Salo sa Sanlo" was indeed a great success and this we partly owe to the active involvement of our volunteers like Dra. Ching Joves as event co-chairwoman, Ms. Chuh Hernandez as overall coordinator and actress/ comedienne Ms. Tessie Tomas.

The people I have mentioned here would surely admit that they too would have not done as well without the earnest support of their peers.

In the same breath, our Barangay could not function effectively well without the diligent and collaborative efforts of our employees. This was aptly put to test just recently as the formidable force of Typhoon Milenyo wreaked havoc on our community streets. In the ensuing clearing operation, our Barangay employees willingly and tirelessly worked extended hours to render our streets immediately passable.

The bottom line is: we all have an idea of the kind of community we want to live in. And we salute our Barangay Volunteers for their willingness to work for that ideal without expectation of any tangible gain. In closing, what comes to my mind is a quote from the great Mahatma Gandhi that "we must be the change we wish to see."

Getting Things Done

Veredigno Atienza

Last October 2006, we successfully converted Linkages the quarterly newspaper into a magazine, initially a quarterly magazine with hopes of making it monthly.

In September 2006, as the first issue of Linkages magazine was being finalized, a wonderful opportunity for a tie-up with the Philippine Daily Inquirer cropped up. We must credit our Assumption College connection for this development. Our BSLBA director Kuku Lopez who is also an Assumption College associate dean, had a chat with (PDI) president Sandy Prieto-Romualdez, and the idea of a tie-up simply came up. With inputs from the Linkages Editorial Board and the BSLBA Board of Directors, a deal was worked out.

This issue of Linkages magazine is a product of the new arrangement with the Inquirer Group. Barangay San Lorenzo will continue to own the magazine; BSLBA will continue with the overall management and distribution of the magazine. We will also ensure implementation of editorial policy, provide content and work closely with the Inquirer Group's Hinge Inquirer Publications (HIP) which will handle editorial, design, layout, printing, and the inevitable and necessary advertising sales.

To complement Linkages, we have established a website, www.bslba.org, which will serve as a portal to BSLBA, to BSL, and to San Lorenzo Village

Association. We thank BSLBA director Jaime Garchitorena, Edupro president and Spinweb Inc., for helping make the website a reality.

We had our first Monthly Business Forum (MBF) at the Bizu restaurant at Greenbelt last October 6, 2006, with PDI columnist and ANC TV host Manuel Quezon as our speaker. His talk delved on constitutional change, modes of constitutional change and their implications on our society, our economy, and business in general.

The next MBF was on January 12, 2007. The topic "No Tax on Work" brought up nontraditional taxation and public finance matters, ie the need for more consumption taxation, less income taxation, more spending on capital expenditures, and less on current expenditures. A February MBF was held with Ayala Foundation president Vicky Garchitorena as speaker. Director-in-charge Liza Guillermo will provide us with speakers for subsequent months.

We are holding the BSL Business Week from March 25 -31, 2007. BSL Business Week will have a two-day Trade Exhibit, the Annual Business Forum and several seminars. Over-all chair for BSL Business Week is BSL Secretary and BSLBA Director Ernie Moya.

The trade exhibit, a vital component of the BSLBA week will feature 32 booths open to the members of the BSL community reflecting the diversity within the community. The exhibit will take place on March 30 and 31 in Glorietta 3. The seminars will cover capital sources for micro-enterprises and SMEs, and the rationale and mechanics of franchising. The annual forum will follow the roundtable format on the topic "In Search of a National Consensus".

With regard to seminars, BSLBA can also be a marketing hub, via revenue-sharing agreements with companies offering their respective seminars and organization development programs. Directors-in-charge Diva Abad Santos and Jaime Garchitorena handle our seminar- related activities.

Considering the various point-of-sale locations in BSL, BSLBA has adopted reusable acrylic plastic boxes as a vehicle for inviting on-the-spot contributions to various not-for-profit, nongovernmental organizations. We are doing a pilot project, involving twenty locations, with the following as beneficiaries: T'Boli, SKAP, PERDISCO, Pugad sa Don Bosco, Make a Wish Foundation, and other related foundations. BSLBA will retain 5% of all collections to cover some costs. Director-in-charge of the Community Outreach Committee is Marlene Po.

During the Monthly Forum where Vicky Garchitorena spoke on corporate social responsibility, BSLBA pledged PP100,000 for GILAS, Ayala's project involving wiring public high schools for the Internet. Last February 17, 2007, BSLBA donated the following to SKAP in Bgy Pembo: a pro-gym, a sandbag, a keyboard, a monitor, and a scanner. BSLBA also secured employment for SKAP members (alternating four at a time) from November 2006 up to March 2007 at an Ortigas call center, with the possibility of an extension.

We have had a substantial increase in membership. Membership now stands at 5,700. We have also organized our membership on a per-block basis. The block reps or block heads will help the Directors-in-charge to execute BSLBA programs, particularly those with special relevance to their blocks. The blocks can have block committees to replicate the BSLBA wide-committees. The director in charge of the Membership Committee is Jess La O'.

The above frontline committees are revenue generators that will provide the wherewithal to BSLBA to make it an effective and efficient association. Given viable and sustainable sources of revenue, BSLBA will be able to organize work in more esoteric areas: the promotion of entrepreneurship, protection of barangay businesses, employment generation, productivity enhancement, inter-barangay business cooperation, development of barangay businessess, and incentives and financial assistance to barangay businesses.

The above committees make use of the services of the central units, namely, the Finance Committee with director-in-charge Jun Santillana, the Media Committee with director-in-charge Ernie Moya and Central Admin with BSLBA president/CEO and acting executive director Vernie Atienza.

My thanks in turn to BSLBA acting executive director Ton Francisco and admin officer Fe Valdez, to the BSLBA board, the council members and staff of Brgy. San Lorenzo and Brgy Chair Jay Santiago. BSLBA Chair Annie Tanchanco will preside over the Annual Membershiip Meeting and the Elections for a new Board.

Indeed we are going to turn over a going concern to the next BSLBA Board.

BSLBA invites one and all to active participation in BSLBA programs. Thank you.

Coming and Going

Veredigno Atienza

On May 31, 2007, I would have ended my term as BSLBA president for the year 2006-2007. The Board of Directors elected me president in June 2006, and by May 31, I would have served for eleven months. What have the past eleven months or so, taught me? One thing clearly stands out: the importance of gratitude, appreciation, generosity, and openness. These traits or characteristics are not exclusive of one another, and tend to correlate closely with one another.

Gratitude is the ability to recognize the contributions of other people, and to be thankful for such contributions. No leader or manager stands alone. He stands on the shoulders of the people who went ahead of him and on the shoulders of the people currently with him.

In my case as BSLBA president, I recognize the support given by Barangay Chairman Joshua John "Jay" Santiago and the members of the Barangay Council. With his support, I got elected president of BSLBA, got the backing of the Board behind my programs, got funding for my action plan, and obtained the mechanism for increasing the membership of BSLBA from 300 to more than 6000.

I likewise must thank former Barangay Secretary Ernie Moya who got me as an incorporator of BSLBA in 2004. During my term as president, Secretary Ernie served as Board Director and member of the Central

Admin Committee. He was also the passion, energy and guiding light behind the successful BSL Business Week held last March 25 to March 31, 2007. For all these, I am grateful to Director Ernie Moya, my friend and college classmate, who by the way loves to tell people I am ten years older than he is.

Appreciation is the ability to recognize the value of the work done by other people even if what they do is simply part of their job.

At the Central Admin Office, two people have proven vital to the day-to-day operations of BSLBA: our Assistant Executive Director Tonton Francisco and Admin Officer Fe Valdez. Tonton has an MBA from the Ateneo Graduate School of Business, great PR, and invaluable persistency. She proved her worth particularly during BSL Business Week, which included six major activities: 1) the Trade Exhibit at Glorietta 3, 2) the Annual Business Forum (Roundtable on "In Search of a National Consensus") at My Cinema, 3) the Small Business Finance Seminar and 4) the Franchising Seminar at the Barangay Hall, 5) the Fun Run, and 6) the Recognition Awards for the Sunday Market Entrepreneurs. In all of these, Fe provided admin support, attending to innumerable details.

Between the two of them, over the past eleven months, they have supported the work of the different BSLBA Committees: Membership and Organization, Linkages Magazine, Monthly Business Forum, Website, Outreach, MIB Card, Education, Finance and Media.

Many other people have helped the BSLBA Central Admin and the BSLBA Committees, and I would like to name all of them if I can (pardon me if I fail to do so): Myrna Fernandez, Pam Perez, Sandy Espinosa, Kate Villasenor, Lito Rivera, Col. Wenceslao Cruz, Lilia Sesperes, Sandy Prieto Romualdez, Vicky Garchitorena, Ramon Arteficio, Susan Roxas-Oshima, Lorie Tan, Fengjiang Liu, Manuel 'Manolo' Quezon, Marinela 'Sam' de Leon, Doris Bermudez, Lisa Villanueva, Rene Azurin, Rolando Dy, Dennis Gonzalez, Billy Esposo, Nonoy Oplas, Bjorn Tarras-Wahlberg, David Stanley, Louie Locsin, Bernardo Lopez, Harry Tambuatco, Lynn Ruiz, Arnold Salvador, Sister Imelda Reposar, Jojo Bunag, Nelson Aspe, Nieva Guerrero, Bobby Mailig, Marissa Rabago-Uy, Nestor Coson, Loida Esquivias, Tony Aluquin, Richard Sudla, Richard Gonzales, Dolly Belgica, Menchie Buna, Benel Lagua, Butch Bartolome, Iwan Soetjahja MD, Winnie Ferrer, Raymond Trajano, Lito Anzures, Mayor Jejomar Binay, Councilor Rodolfo Sese, Frankie Roman, Jaime Garchitorena, Fr. Emil Santos, Joel Amante, Andi Requintina, Brenda del Rosario, Denver Trinidad, Yeye Querubin, Joy Tapiador, Rose Malano, Ching Joves, Verna Tan, Jane Roque, Glenda Velasco, Rebecca Estavillo, Glenn Tengco, Kristalyn Reloto, Cathy Peralta, Marvie Esponilla, Dondon Ursua, Gilbert Roda, Eleanor Juliano, Marlon Tandoc, Michelle Ramiscal, Adrian Samaniego, Gary Co, Mara de Tavera, Gene Fabregas, Mylene Mariano, Lito Banawa, Sheila Ang Enriquez, Belen Bactad, Norma Cruz, Lita de los Nieves, Ma. Cristina Garcia, Ched Topacio, Sonny Galanga, John Achaval, Tessa Tayag, Jimmy Biglang-Awa, Lito Quiogue, Kath del Rosario, Norman Golez, Dean de la Paz, Jack Wong, Gino Bolos, Beth Ona, Dero Pedero, Ariel Tapang Lopez.

Generosity is the willingness to share one's resources, be it talent, time, connections, funding, experience, education, emotional strength. Generosity begets generosity. As indicated above, while we have shared resources with others, they too have shared resources with us. In an ever-widening loop of generosity, much has been achieved for BSLBA and for the community at large. Our two-year old organization is where it is because of the generosity of many people, but most especially our Board of Directors: Jesse LaO', Jun Santillana, Liza Guillermo, Marlene Po (now Barangay Secretary), Kuku Lopez, BSLBA Chair Annie Tanchanco, and the BSL ex-officio directors Chair Jay Santiago, Kagawad Diva Abad-Santos, and former Secretary Ernie Moya.

Openness is the driver of the above traits. It takes openness to be grateful, appreciative, and generous. It takes openness to let others take the credit. An open person is open to the ideas and contributions of other people. An open person is willing to listen and is genuinely interested in others as persons not as mere stepping-stones or factors of production. An open person is open to new friends and to new relationships, even though there is always a built-in risk in letting people into one's life. There is always the downside risk of hurt, disappointment, betrayal, pain, separation and loss.

Gratitude, appreciation, generosity, openness. They are refinements of the heart. May there be more people with gratitude, appreciation, generosity, and openness involved in the affairs of BSLBA.

As the year peters out, much remains to be done: improvement of what we have started this year and of what we have carried on from the first year, and new initiatives such as the carbon credit anti-global warming program, a tie-up with the Management Association of the Philippines on "Bambis" (otherwise known as Barangay Micro Enterprise Program), a BSL-wide health plan for low-income employees (maids, waiters, clerks, janitors, sales girls, guards, drivers, et al), and an employment assistance program for the disabled.

Best wishes to the incoming Board and officers, Committee chairs and members, bloc reps, and industry reps. Our dear members, please get involved and make your presence felt by all. You are most welcome to do so. Mabuhay kayong lahat.

SECTION THREE: PRIVATE ENTERPRISE

Chimara: a Neo Vegan Lifestyle for All

Annie Tanchanco

Banishing the notion that vegetarianism is only for the spiritual, elderly fashion models, health buffs and animal rights activists, Chimara Neo Vegan Café in Greenbelt 3 has been attracting crowds of ordinary folks who keep coming back for more of its unique, delicious and healthy fare.

When it first opened in 2002, Chimara became well known for healthy versions of popular movie treats like olive oil-popped popcorn, vacuum processed chips, flavored seasonings, and their best seller tofu chips. The cafe is after all, strategically located beside the cinemas and a sister company of the country's leading snack chain, Taters.

In three years, Chimara has gathered a hefty number of followers who are just addicted to its wide range of meal offerings that include soups, salads, pita wraps, pita romanas, rice dishes and smoothies. It even introduced the first and only soy ice cream in the Philippine market.

Chimara comes from the Greek word "chimera", which means "an impossible dream". Greek thinkers philosophize that "each one of us dreams of a healthy, harmonious and sustainable life but lacks initiative in acting on it."

"All you have to do is take a small step by enjoying our nude food, and this life becomes your reality." Chimara describes their food as nude, meaning free from preservatives and additives and over-processing – a creative twist.

Chimera promotes itself to health buffs and vegetarians, but mostly to non-vegetarians who never had the chance to eat our healthy fare. Calling customers "neovegans," Chimera does not discriminate as to strict "vegans" or "vegetarians." In fact, 80% of customers are non-vegetarians who just love the scrumptious healthy food.

Chimara has the yummiest protein-packed salads in town. Chimara offers a lot of soy and tofu in its menu. The café is proud to be the first to introduce Soy Ice Cream (a healthy, low fat, lactose free, protein-rich alternative that we have in the market), which is an in-house formulation. It's certainly worth trying. Chimara will even be coming out with sugar-free flavors.

Thirst quenchers include fresh fruit juices, soy smoothies, soy milk and green tea. Begin or end your day with a healthy cup of Soy Coffee. For caffeine lovers, Organic Barako Coffee is available.

Due to popular demand, Chimara delivers around the Makati area. Even South Beach diet fans love Chimara. A customer who was in the phase 2 of her South Beach Diet said she prefers Chimara as her diet food. "So much less expensive but so much more tasty!" she enthused. This is probably one of the main reasons why the delivery service is so successful.

More than anything, it is Chimara's almost utopian philosophy that adds passion and meaning to Chimara's advocacy. They believe that to instigate change, change must come from within.

Thus, the café encourages the use of recyclable, reusable products, organic GMO-free ingredients, and part of their sales is allotted to help the Center of Excellence in Public Elementary Education. One percent of the customer's purchase in Chimara, goes to CENTEX, an Ayala Foundation project tasked to provide scholarships to bright and promising, less fortunate kids.

Entrepreneur/Intrapreneur: Jaime Garchitorena

Ma. Wivina Ferrer

Jaime Garchitorena- The name rang a bell. I had seen him in the BSLBA annual membership meeting. His departed father Justice Francis Garchitorena was a good friend of my father.

He joined EDUPRO two years ago, and this company just turned ten years the day before this interview. He explained that EDUPRO is a Microsoft Partner for learning. One does not have to be an IT Professional to be able to understand the modules.

Edupro belongs to the NEXUS Group of Companies which ranks 700 in the top 1,000 companies globally. The Jupiter System, a software development company in Asia, and WSI which ranks 900 in the Philippine top 1000 companies, are part of NEXUS. EDUPRO is the training outlet for the three companies.

When questioned on his ownership, his answer was yes and no. "I don't own the company but my prerequisite in joining one is that I be given the reins, meaning I will run the company as if it were my own. The only thing I will not do is to sign checks." In the case of EDUPRO he reviewed the business model (education as a business) and he concluded that it will make money. Just like any product it is a matter of "brand positioning."

When he talked about his past experience, he casually mentioned his eight (8) years with pharmaceuticals, which ended when his personal relationship ended. "We both worked hard at it. We were creative in managing the circumstances, working with a minimal budget."

After this, he did nothing for two years, at the end of which he decided to enroll at the Asian Institute of Management where he took up entrepreneurship.

He says that he is strict with people. He doesn't believe in excuses such as no budget. "One can always find ways," he quips.

The key to success is to recognize where you're good at and work with what you have. It is very rare that one person can possess all the attributes, so build a team where one's deficiencies may be compensated by another's strengths or skill.

According to Jaime, a true entrepreneur must be able to balance formal education and experiential learning. He must be able to see what no one else can, and be able to act on what he sees. He cites the budding entrepreneur who has a 9-5 job. The job takes care of his vision. Quietly he keeps working on his skills, translates them into earnings and savings, and when he has honed his special skills and has saved enough, that's when he becomes an entrepreneur.

The dictionary meaning of an entrepreneur is a revolutionary, a rebel. He must be willing to sacrifice. The key to success includes the ability to honestly assess oneself. "Do I have the product, the skill? One shouldn't be afraid to say, 'No, I don't.' If you believe in yourself, you will find a way. One must be ready to push onwards."

SECTION FOUR: OUTREACH

Don Bosco Pugad Home for Street Children: a Place for Caring

Marlene Po

"Don Bosco Pugad Home for Street Children and Migrant Youth" in Barangay San Lorenzo is a place of healing, caring and teaching. Character-building is done by St. John Bosco's system of reason, religion and kindness, to prevent them from going back to the streets.

Immediate reconstruction of value systems damaged by street culture is given priority. Pugad is a home that welcomes, a school that prepares the boys for life, a playground that fosters and encourages friendships, and a church that accompanies them in their journey thru life.

The Don Bosco Pugad Home was founded and established by the Salesians of Don Bosco. Currently handling around 90 youths staying in the center, it caters mainly to boys aged 6-18 years old who belong to the Drop-In Sector and 17-24 years old who are categorized in the Migrant Youth Sector.

The center also offers a homecare program, alternative education, a psychological and psycho-spiritual program, health services, skills training and even after-care services. Livelihood programs include bakery training, coffee shop operations, water refilling, orchid-selling and tocino-making.

Making Wishes Come True

Marlene Po

Christian Lanzar, a hemophilia-stricken child, wanted to sing to the world.

On New Year's Eve 1999, his wish was granted. Together with pop diva Regine Velasquez, by the fountain of the Manila Peninsula Hotel, he sang during the global broadcast of the special millennium program.

This was the very first wish granted in the Philippines by Make-A-Wish Foundation, which wish eventually won the Best Wish of the Year International. Since then, over 600 terminally-ill children have seen their wishes come true.

Make-a-Wish Foundation International was started in 1980 in the United States when a seven-year old leukemia sufferer, Christopher Grecius, expressed his desire of being a policeman for a day. Friends, family and their community in Arizona rallied together to provide Chris with an unforgettable experience. In a uniform, he was sworn in as an officer of the law, was issued his badge, went on patrol, rode in a police helicopter and a motorcycle.

In the past 25 years, 30 countries have granted more than 120,000 wishes, ranging from a simple Barbie doll request to the more complex ones, such as meeting a head of state.

In the Philippines, Make A Wish Foundation has already granted over 600 wishes in its six-year stint. It is currently headed by Kahlil Bagatsing, managing director of Channel Card Convergence and a part-time university professor.

Recounting how he became involved in this advocacy, he explains that he was supposed to join Make a Wish San Francisco when his father asked him to return to the Philippines to help with the family business.

"I wasn't aware that there was Make a Wish in the Philippines. A couple of months after I got back, I met the Marketing Director and she mentioned that there was a local chapter and I have been involved ever since, "Bagatsing recalled.

Granting a child's wish could be one of the most moving experiences in one's lifetime.

"I am a firm believer that there are certain cures that are beyond the realm of medical science. Sometimes all these kids need is someone to believe in them. It's just amazing to know that a simple act has the potential to help turn a life around," he added.

The Foundation receives between five to ten wishes a month. When a family member, friend, or a hospital staff refers a child; the type and severity of the illness, and the names of the physicians and of the hospital are submitted to the wish Referral Committee, which then consults the list of ailments that could qualify the child to be a wish kid.

If eligible, the child is interviewed on his/her set of wishes, and is asked to rank them in order of importance and to sort them into categories such as "I wish to have...," "I wish to be...," "I wish to go...," and "I wish to meet."

To date, the most popular wishes are to have a computer, a Playstation 2, a Gameboy, a TV set or a mobile phone. The more elaborate ones include meeting President Gloria Macapagal-Arroyo or a trip to Disneyland.

The Foundation, however, is not just about finding and screening wish kids and making their dreams come true. It is also about making ordinary folks realize that they could make a positive contribution to other people's lives, even in seemingly small ways.

Quoting Lawrence and Anj L., individual sponsors: "Thank you for allowing us to experience the joy of giving. We hope that in the future we'll be able to help more cancer kids, as their desire to LIVE is our inspiration."

To nurture its growing base of supporters, the Foundation started the Adopt A Wish Program to encourage people to be involved in its cause.

By tapping schools, parishes, village associations and companies as partners, it hopes to build a network of supporters for various wishes: from conceptualization and gathering of donations to the actual grant of the wishes.

Bagatsing enjoins everyone to join their cause and help share the power of a wish. "Make A Wish is about joy, strength, and hope."

Giving the Smile Back to Street Children

Virlanie Foundation, Inc.

In 2001, a fourteen-year-old boy called Joseph found himself in the streets of Manila after escaping from his home in Laguna. He was one of the many street children, managing to keep his body and soul together by scraping a living selling mineral water in the street. He slept badly at night, in any shelter he could find – often waking up to make sure he wasn't in danger of being robbed or hurt. He was receiving no formal education, not eating a proper diet and had no hope for a better future.

During that year, a helping hand was extended when Joseph met "Ate Marie Virlanie". This lady, whose name is familiar to many current and former children of the streets, is one of the Street Educators of Virlan Foundation, Inc (VFI), the largest private non-sectarian child caring institution in Metro Manila, Philippines. Ate Marie persuaded Joseph to leave the streets and enter the care of the foundation.

VFI operates twelve residential homes providing shelter, food, education and love to street children and child prostitutes. These are set up to mirror the structure of a traditional Filipino family and no house contains more than thirty children. VFI also operates support programs that cater to their personal development, including a learning center, a creative and development center, a family reunification program and a program catering to career development and guidance for young adults.

One outreach program, the Street Education Program, works with children in the community, seeking to alleviate poverty and fight injustice.

An office works in the field of legal rights of children in conflict with the law. Another program combats problems of child labor, poor education, malnutrition, child abuse and child trafficking in the poorer communities of Metro Manila. VFI also runs a volunteer program and facilitates individual sponsorship from local and foreign benefactors of children both in the VFI homes and in the poorer communities of Manila.

Joseph found himself in one of VFI's transitory homes for new arrivals, before being transferred to one of the long-term homes. He started to go school, and to learn to use computers from one of the volunteers. He also learned to play the drums and the guitar, and played basketball in district tournaments. VFI places emphasis on being part of the community and on distilling in the children a sense of citizenship, and thus Joseph began to dream of an independent and sustainable future for himself.

In 2003 Joseph registered with VFI's Young Adult Program to receive training and guidance regarding his future career. He participated in seminars on life planning, team building, personal relationships and communicating efficiently. In 2004 he got his first job – working as a waiter in an office building. Today, he is a waiter in one of Manila's upmarket malls. He is very proud to be working there and now lives independently in a small apartment very near the foundation.

Run by a dedicated team of 100 Filipino staff members and assisted by around twenty-five volunteers, both Filipino and foreign, VFI has helped thousands of children like Joseph since it was founded in 1992. Some of the children come directly from the street, and others are referred from other institutions.

VFI ensures that the children receive appropriate residential, medical, social, psychological, psychiatric, educational, spiritual, sports and recreational services and above all, that they receive love. It also works to change the mindsets of those with the power to effect change regarding the rights of children; and to empower the poorer communities in Manila to break the cycle of poverty.

VFI is grateful for any type of assistance, financial donations, sponsorship, technical expertise or offers of internships for young adults. It welcomes volunteers to give tutorials, facilitate activities and outings for the children, work as street educators, give seminars to young adults, raise funds, and publicize its work or help in one of VFI's many other essential areas of activity.

What is Rock Ed?

Jaime Garchitorena

Rock Ed is a 10-year series of projects that focus on the eight millennium development goals as defined by the United Nations. The eight are: eradication of extreme poverty and hunger, universal primary education, gender equality and women empowerment, reduction of child mortality, improvement of maternal health, combat HIV/AIDS, malaria and other diseases, environmental sustainability, and the development of a Global Partnership for Development.

Rock Ed works to develop awareness for these eight millennium development goals through various alternative education methods, basically art forms and non-traditional media like concerts, art exhibits, poetry reading sessions, and art classes.

Why does there seem to be an emphasis on alternative methods of communicating these development goals?

The main target with these methods is obviously the youth. We want to present what might normally be boring, though relevant, topics to them in a method that holds the best possibility of absorption and understanding. This is not a new concept at all. The teachers we learn from and remember the best are usually the ones who use innovative ways of teaching. Usually an interesting manner of speaking or a purposeful use of visual aids helped in the learning process.

Can you give us an example of a project using these alternative methods?

Last December 10th we celebrated World Human Rights Day through Rock da Riles. Rock da Riles had different art forms, ie poetry reading, mural painting, story telling and music at the different MRT stations. Each station represented a millennium development goal. For example, the Makati station represented the environment and we had a concert there with different bands playing.

How effective was that event in communicating the concerns about the environment?

 We partnered with other groups directly related to the environment. They had booths with projected visuals and asked people to sign up for their various events or causes. Rock-Ed had a signup station too and the number of sign-ups was significant. Makati is a very busy station and to hold people's attention enough to stop them and make them ask questions about things they might normally not care about is mostly due to the concerts and the great visuals they saw.

So as effective as the program is when Rock-Ed delivers it, how easy is it to adopt and duplicate?

It's easy enough. It requires just two things; one is that you know who you're communicating the message to and two is that you have to get creative in trying to catch their attention. It's very similar to any marketing and advertising program where the message has to fit the market and the medium has to match the market.

Since BSLBA is composed primarily of businessmen, how can they get involved in Rock-Ed's cause?

Rock-Ed is an interesting model because rather than shoehorn a group or an individual into various projects, we prefer that they find a project, hopefully based on any of the 8 millennium development goals, that they can really sink their teeth into. It's important that the project means something to them if it is to be effective.

In the case of businessmen in Makati who may have the resources but not the time, they can adopt a millennium development goal and work their inter-office activities around this theme. For example during company outings this summer, since companies like to do outdoor activities, they can theme their projects. For example, a trip to a beach resort might have a small lecture on the marine environment and how to preserve it.

The combination of being at the beach and understanding man's effect on the waters in which he is about to swim in, can have more impact than just an audio visual presentation in a cold Makati office.

Story telling sessions for the employee's children focusing on themes of good conduct as a Filipino or even something as simple as naming the inter-office basketball teams with relevant names in history to create an awareness of our historical past can be ways of bringing back a sense of national pride. The options for action are really endless and they are not bound by financial issues. The important thing is that the message can fit into the medium and the medium is relevant and interesting to the target audience.

In case these companies need help in finding the resources to create programs that have relevance, they can always email us at rockedphilippines@yahoo.com and we can help them create the framework and the activities for delivering the message.

Any final message to our readers?

Bottom line is get involved. Find a cause that fits your personality and run with it. The great thing is that when people see you involved and enjoying it, it becomes infectious and the scope of influence that we create becomes wider and more significant.

Salupa

Kath del Rosario

SEVERAL weeks after Joshua John Santiago took his oath as Barangay San Lorenzo Chairman, he personally talked with the informal settlers of Urban Botanical Garden, headed then by now Barangay Treasurer Rose Malano for a project that would help the latter.

The talk ended in an agreement to organize an NGO (non-governmental organization) now known as SALUPA or San Lorenzo Urban Poor Association Makati City, Inc.

To formalize and make it more stable, SALUPA was officially registered at the Security and Exchange Commission as the recognized NGO of informal settlers in Barangay San Lorenzo.

SALUPA's first president was Rose Malano and succeeded by Edith Bonifacio recently. There are 180 families plus bedspacers and other renters for more or less 1,000 residents.

"Actually wala pang 50 pamilya noon, ngayon 180 na ang pamilyang naninirahan dito," Rose said where 40 percent are employed and the rest (60 percent) are all students or youths.

Before SALUPA, the Urban Botanical Garden was a chapter of Bayanihan para sa Salinlahi, an NGO based in Quezon City.

"Ako yung nakaisip ng SALUPA," Rose continued, "Kasi before naming i-organize ito, ang main objective namin ay land tenure. We are fighting for our rights sa lupa not necessarily na hindi kami ma-evict dito but yung mga karapatan ng mga tao na magkaroon ng bahay na titirahan. **Pagka may organization, may unity, may puwersa, hindi watak-watak."**

"Nung ipinaramdam sa amin ni Kapitan Jay Santiago na kahit narito kami sa ganitong lugar eh pare-parehas lang ang lahat ng mga tao, we decided na talagang kasama nga kami sa Barangay San Lorenzo."

The group admitted that at first, they felt inferior because of the different lifestyles they have. However, this was erased under the leadership of Mr. Santiago who helped them and gave them proper training to uplift their standard of living.

"Ready na kami. Tanggap na namin na hindi ito ang permanent residence namin. Temporary lang ang pag-i-stay namin dito. Sa panahon ngayon dapat maging realistic ka."

"Yung mga training na ipinagkaloob sa amin ng libre ay talagang malaking tulong. Kahit mawala ang SALUPA, yung mga training na nai-share sa amin ng San Lorenzo ang aming magiging puhunan," she said.

"Kahit ang mga anak namin ay sumailalim na rin sa iba't ibang training," Bonifacio added, referring to livelihood programs like bead making, computer courses like encoding and layouting; and waitering and bartending.

These livelihood programs, also known as learn-to-earn programs, were not only for the youth but for adults as well. Cosmetology, candle making and soap making were offered to housewives to help in augmenting the family income while technical training was offered to all "padres de pamilya".

"Kung pakakawalan na ang mga tao sa Botanical, I am sure makakatayo na sila," said the former SALUPA president.

Having SALUPA under Barangay San Lorenzo is such a blessing to all the residents there.

"Unang-unang nabago rito ay peace and order and cleanliness. Nabura na naming yung image na pag sa ganitong klase ka nakatira eh narito na ang lahat ng bisyo. Hindi porke nasa marginalized sector kami ng lipunan eh ganoon na nga kami."

"Mula ng ma-organize ang SALUPA, nabawasan ang away, nawala ang inuman sa kalsada. Ipinagbawal talaga namin yun."

SALUPA maintains marshals for Botanical, a special project of Barangay San Lorenzo, for the peace and order. Even the residents themselves decided to support the marshals by imposing a fine to offenders and a seven-day curfew to all youths in the area.

"Mahigpit naming pinapa-implement ang curfew from 10 p.m. to 4 a.m. araw-araw. Me pumipito na marshal kapag sumapit na ang alas-10 ng gabi at makikita mo na talagang nagmamadaling umuwi yung mga kabataan dito. Kapag may nahuli kami, ipinapatawag namin ang magulang at kinakausap."

Every summer, SALUPA organizes sports festival to make the residents, especially the youth, stay away from drugs. SALUPA claims that there are no beggars in their area. Their biggest contribution is keeping Botanical clean.

"Very proud si Kap na name-maintain namin ang cleanliness dito. Wala ring nabibiktima dito ng bukas kotse, snatching, o holdaper. I can assure them. Hindi ko masasabing 100 percent safe pero kung me naganap na ganoon, hindi taga-Botanical ang gagawa noon."

"Kaya naming sabihin sa buong Pilipinas na ang Botanical ay maraming benefits and privileges galing sa barangay. Meron kaming libreng flu vaccine, feeding program at isinasama nila kami sa kanilang Halloween party."

"Me libre kaming gamot at kapag Christmas ang daming giveaways. Yung streetlights sila rin ang nagbabayad ng monthly bill, kasi alam nilang hindi namin kaya (financially)," the group explained further. As of now, the barangay is helping them get their own water connection.

"Kaya napakaswerte namin na yung lugar na napuntahan namin ay sakop ng Barangay San Lorenzo."

In return, people in Botanical through SALUPA's assistance, have tried very hard to cooperate and help the barangay.

"Very cooperative ang mga tao rito dahil nahihiya kami ke Kap. May personal touch kasi siya sa tao.

Hindi siya nakakahiyang lapitan. Pina-feel niya sa tao na siya eh puwedeng bumaba sa amin."

"Si Mam Diva (Kag. Diva Abad Santos) talagang active din ever since."

Though they admitted that they lack the funds, they came up with alternatives in order not to let Brgy. Chair Santiago down, and helped him prove that organizing SALUPA was not a mistake but an advantage.

A Taste of T'boli in the City: Giving Indigenous Artists a Chance

Marlene Po

Foreign stars (or even mere upstarts) in the worlds of ballet, opera, classical music, jazz, pop and rock have been feted, toasted and applauded. Yet right in our own backyard we have grossly overlooked even denigrated indigenous artistic virtuosity and talent.

In Lake Sebu South Cotabato, the Helobung Cultural Troupe is alive and preparing for their first ever full-length solo show in Manila – coming, ironically, after their overseas sold-out gala at the Brava Theater, San Francisco in 2003.

On November 24, 2006 at Equitable PCIBank's Francisco Santiago Hall, indigenous artists will be given a chance to shine, offering us an extraordinary opportunity to savor a rich sampling of T'boli music and dances by a collective of twelve indigenous T'boli master artists. The artists will share their repertoire of a traditional and continuously dynamic cultural legacy where identity and education are constantly formulated, shared, and preserved as well as deconstructed, revised and reborn.

Beginnings

The Helobung – which means "endless joy" in T'boli, was formed in 1986 when several young T'bolis recognized the need to safeguard their rich heritage. Thus, community elders have since been encouraged to teach the younger members of the community traditional skills in agriculture, healing, weaving, embroidery, brass casting and other visual arts.

On the other hand, it is through the Helobung Troupe that cultural stewardship and creativity are expressed through the performing arts, a valuable lens through which to explore issues of identity and a channel to promote individual self-affirmation and community empowerment.

Their Dances

The T'bolis, an indigenous people of Southern Philippines renowned for their t'nalak weaving and elaborate and colorful attires, celebrate the complex beauty of tribal life and their spiritual relationship with their land through music and movement.

The Helobung will interpret the Legend of Lake Sebu, where Boi Henwu - the first woman created by D'wata (Supreme Deity) - turns over a takul leaf under which spurts forth the waters of Lake Sebu.

In the Lenakaw, the Dance of the Lunar Eclipse, a python devours the fairest village lass. In the Kadalliwas, dancers follow a relentless beat, mimicking a bunch of monkeys removing nits and lice from each other. In one courtship dance, a boy pursues a girl, who taunts him with an unfurled kayab or turban or the kadal herayon whereby "flirting gestures" would express what a girl otherwise cannot say.

It is extremely interesting to note that, although its members promote and advocate for T'boli culture, they also express their views about how certain age-old practices can be harmful, like arranged marriages. Their choice of repertoire likewise raises awareness about current issues and challenges that they face, such as the struggle to regain their ancestral land and the threats to their environment.

Their Music

Their show will make us appreciate the depth and range of T'boli music   since all visiting artists are highly skilled at playing a variety of instruments, like the tnonggong, a drum from bamboo and stretched monkey skin; the sloli, a bamboo flute; and the kumbing, a mouth harp which is used more frequently by men for short distance courtship. Handier, cheaper and definitely more romantic than texting, it is said that the intimate language of love and lovemaking can easily be expressed through this simple and lightweight bamboo instrument.

The sludoy, a bamboo zither, is used during the day when the player is lighthearted or when a visitor is being welcomed.   The hegelung, a long, slender, and spindle-shaped two-stringed lute, has frets made of lefak wood and covered in beeswax taken from the songko, the smallest type of bees. The T'bolis believe that by rubbing their fingers with the leaves of the meglung vine and a long-legged insect, also called meglung, they can learn to play since rhyming names (meglung and hegelung) are perceived to be effective in acquring skills.

The T'bolis are also adept in playing the kulintang, a set of 8 graduated laid-out brass gongs. The blowon, on the other hand, are large hanging gongs. One instance in which it is used is when wedding guests from the groom's side, walking towards the girl's house, start striking the blowon as a signal of their approach, since the sound can be heard from quite a distance.

The Artists

Guests will be privileged to watch Maria Wanan, Helobung Executive Director and a highly skilled dancer, musician (kulintang, blowon, tnonggong) and chanter. She performed at the 1994 Phillippine Festival of Arts in Paris, the 1998 Thirty-Second Smithsonian American Folktale Festival and the 1998 Philippine Centennial celebration: Pahiyas, both in Washington D.C.

Rosie Sula is a powerful luningon chanter, a hegelung player and a dancer. A community organizer and one of the strongest T'boli cultural activists today, she believes that education for the T'boli youth is the key to the conservation of their traditions.

According to his peers, Danilo Kasaw is the best blowon player that the T'boli people have ever produced and documented. He has created a number of percussive music pieces which he alone can execute with speed and rhythmic intricacy. He is regarded by the community as a master musician.

Joel Ganlal, another expert musician, is one of the few who can play the sloli and dwegey as well as the tnonggong. He has performed in Germany.

In all, the audience will embark on an extraordinary journey into the "Tales, Tunes and Threads of the T'bolis".

Sanlo Perdisco

Elizabeth Ona

On February 6 this year, we received a circular that greatly intrigued my husband and me. It said that Barangay San Lorenzo and San Lorenzo Village Association, with the assistance of Architect Jaime Silva, President of the Federation of Persons with Disabilities in Makati, are forming a group to address the many concerns of persons with disabilities (PWD) in Barangay San Lorenzo.

As the mother of a young man diagnosed to be borderline autistic and mildly mentally retarded, that information was a most welcome development. As far as I know, this was the first time that such an effort was being made. So it was with enthusiasm mingled with curiosity that we attended the first meeting of a small group composed of PWDs, their parents, guardians and caregivers under the trees of the San Lorenzo Village Park.

At that first meeting and the others that followed, we got to know each other better as we shared our experiences and the challenges we have met in raising our "special children". I thought that our gatherings would merely be just bonding and networking sessions. We even resisted the idea of forming ourselves into a formal group with sets of officers. I should have known better.

Present at those initial meetings were our dynamic Punong Barangay Jay Santiago and the enthusiastic

Architect Silva, whose blind condition did not seem to hamper his determination to form as many groups as he can of PWDs in Makati especially in the so-called exclusive villages. These two movers and doers believed that the PWDs must be united into a strong force so that their plight can no longer be ignored.

As we continued to meet every first Friday of the month, it soon became clear to us that they were right. We really need a set of officers to give direction to our group in achieving our goal, which is: to help the PWDs improve the quality of their lives by being productive, independent and useful participants in the community. And it would also be nice if in the process we could give them some occasions for laughter and fun. Why not?

So on 13 June 2006 our group elected its first set of officers. I was given the unenviable job of being its president. Our immediate task was to get our group recognized. A name and logo-making contest was launched to raise awareness in the community of the existence of our organization. Up till then the working name of our group was Barangay San Lorenzo Persons with Disabilities Support Group.

The name that accompanied the winning logo was "Barangay San Lorenzo Persons with Disabilities & Co." or "SanLo PerDisCo" for short. We decided to use "& Co." instead of "Support Group" (which seems to highlight the helplessness of the PWDs) in order to put the emphasis on the PWDs themselves rather than on their supporters - parents, relatives, and benefactors. In the new name "Persons with Disabilities & Co.", the first group takes the lead role leaving the supporting role to the latter. The term "Co." is not spelled out as it could mean either company or companions, depending on the reader's interpretation.

The winning logo looks like a house. The roof means that Barangay San Lorenzo shelters and cares for its Persons with Disabilities, represented by PWD in broad letters - P in orange, and D in red. The white space inside the letters P and D look like an access ramp for wheelchairs. The figures with linked hands forming the W in green serve as representation of the slogan **"TOGETHER WE ARE ABLE"**.

With a set of officers, a name and a logo, our group was ready for take off. Sanlo PerDisCo was formally inaugurated on 17 July in an affair that saw the induction of its officers and the unveiling of its logo. The highlight of the evening was the distribution of the Makati PWD ID Card Plus, which entitles the holder to transportation discounts and other benefits that will be given by the City of Makati. The cards were handed out by Ms. Marjorie de Veyra, head of the Makati Social Welfare Department.

In attendance were Barangay San Lo Punong Barangay Jay Santiago and other members of the BSL Council; officers of BSLBA led by Chair Annie Tanchanco and President Bernie Atienza; President Rose Sibug as well as other officers of the BSL Seniors; and family members of PerDisCo PWDs, who all wore t-shirts bearing the group's logo.

To solidify PerDisCo's legal standing, it was registered with the Department of Social Welfare and with Securities and Exchange Commission in the first week of September. Its Articles of Incorporation states that the group aims:

1. To protect the rights and promote the interests of the Persons with Disabilities in Barangay San Lorenzo (PWDs);

2. To enable the PWDs to achieve their highest potential and to fully participate in society;

3. To assist the parents, guardians, families, and caregivers of the PWDs in their efforts to protect, promote, and ensure the rights and well-being of the PWDs;

4. To tap the good will and resources of the City Government of Makati, Barangay San Lorenzo, and other interested persons and organizations on behalf of the PWDs; and

5. To see to it that the benefits of Republic Act No. 7277 (An act providing for the rehabilitation, self-development and self-reliance of disabled persons and their integration into the mainstream of society and for other purposes) and its Implementing Rules and Regulations, are fully availed of by the PWDs.

Many things have happened since PerDisCo's inception early this year. We had a fun time at Timezone , Glorietta 4, courtesy of its president and general manager, Mr. Raffy Pratts, Jr and Barangay Chair Jay Santiago. For some of our PWDs this was their first time at Timezone, which was not surprising, since most of them spend their time confined to their homes. But what really surprised me was that for the PWDs and their companions who come from the informal settlers' community of Urban Botanical (just across from Makati Medical Center), this was their first time to set foot at the Glorietta!

Our indigent PWDs were also given discounted eye examinations and free frames courtesy of the Abesamis Eye Clinic through Dr. Carmen Abesamis-Dichoso, an ophthalmologist who specializes in pediatric eye refraction. Barangay San Lorenzo has also given us a free stall at the Legazpi Sunday market. We plan to start selling on the first Sunday of October. To prepare for this, we have conducted workshops on items we are going to sell like gift paper bags, and bead works, and food products. These workshops were held in a room in the Barangay Hall set aside for the various activities of PerDisCo.

The most promising development so far is the collaboration of Barangay San Lorenzo with the Independent Living Learning Center in a joint project called "Living Independently in Nurturing Communities" (LINC). (see related article)

Through this project, which needs the support and backing of the members of BSLBA for its successful implementation, we hope that our long neglected persons with disabilities will be given a chance to help themselves and to find their place in the community. PerDisCo's slogan is "Together We Are Able". Through Project LINC, the business community can help "enable the disabled."

Project Linc

Elizabeth Ona

Mindful of the need of persons with disabilities (PWDs) to live meaningful lives, parents of PWDs, the PWDs themselves, and concerned members of the Barangay San Lorenzo community formed the San Lorenzo Persons with Disabilities and Co. (Sanlo Perdisco).

The group facilitated the partnership between Barangay San Lorenzo (BSL) and Independent Living Learning Centre (ILLC), a learning institution that aims to maximize the potentials of PWDs through education and paramedical intervention. BSL and ILLC have agreed to collaborate to ensure the successful implementation of a joint project entitled "Living Independently in Nurturing Communities" (LINC).

This project primarily endeavors to improve the quality of life of PWDs in Barangay San Lorenzo and possibly those in other communities. To formalize this collaboration, a memorandum of agreement was signed by the Hon. Joshua John Santiago and Prof. Abelardo Apollo David Jr. of BSL and ILLC, respectively, on August 8, 2006 at the Barangay San Lorenzo Hall. Present at the event were Sanlo Perdisco president Mrs. Elizabeth Ona and members of the Barangay Council.

One of the programs of Project LINC is the Work Training Program, designed to equip PWDs with appropriate behavior and skills necessary for the competent performance of tasks in the work environment. It seeks to enable the PWDs to contribute to their families and society through their employment in a sheltered workshop or in an actual work setting in the community.

Starting August 9, a series of surveys was implemented to identify the possible candidates for the program. A screening process was implemented to identify these individuals' strengths and areas for improvement. To date, five PWDs from San Lorenzo Village, three from Legaspi Village, and six PWDs from the Urban Botanical area have been screened and selected.

With the support of the Barangay San Lorenzo Business Association, and other organizations, qualified PWDs may have more opportunities for gainful employment. Prior to work placement, the PWDs will undergo training by an occupational therapist and/or special education (sped) professional to ensure that work behavior and skills necessary for employment are acquired. Conferences with the PWD and his/her family will be held to ascertain that an appropriate match has been made between the PWD's skills and the job's demands.

A sheltered workshop to be situated at the Barangay San Lorenzo Hall will be opened for PWDs who require a more controlled work environment. Jobs that will be subcontracted from companies such as bagging, wrapping, boxing, sorting, collating, stuffing, and simple assembling will be performed at the sheltered workshop.

Project LINC also envisions eventually developing and implementing play and therapy services for children with developmental conditions, and pertinent rehabilitation services for adults with disabilities.

Do your share to make this vision a reality. Businessmen may outsource jobs to be performed by PWDs in the sheltered workshops or they may offer jobs in their establishments. Allied medical professionals and educators may volunteer their services in the rehabilitation clinic. Members of the community may volunteer to facilitate tasks in the sheltered workshop or give play activities to the children.

Let us all enable the PWDs to help themselves, their families, and the community.

SECTION FIVE: BUSINESS TALK

From Kuku's Nest: Sightings and Sensings

Ma. Corazon "Kuku" T. Lopez

In a recent seminar hosted by the Bureau of Agricultural Research which focused on technology in relation to agriculture and fisheries, I was asked to talk about the topic **"Knowledge Management Strategies in the Promotion of Agriculture and Fisheries Research and Development: Views from the Private Sector and Business Community"**. I would like to think this seminar is one of the many attempts by the scientific community to reach out and connect with the business community.

In my talk I posited two major stands. First: that the efforts regarding agriculture and fisheries research and development must not stop at **promotions alone**. Such efforts must include focused and intensified activities that will lead to the **adoption** of Research & Development outputs to the benefit of the end-users, especially the business community whose profitability can be a catalyst for economic growth.

The second – and which was the main focus of my talk - was that **there is a great divide between the agriculture and fisheries R&D efforts and the demands of the private sector and business community**. Therefore, the main strategic intervention required for knowledge management toward the promotion and adoption of agriculture and fisheries R& D outputs is **to bridge that great divide**.

Those in development management have pointed out that in most countries, the difficulties with the transfer of agricultural technologies from the lab to the fields or the manufacturing facilities are endemic and have not been solved by making extension services more available, which in the case, of the Philippines remains to be very inadequate.

I told the body that I will not bore them with my own interpretation or do a rehash of research materials, which can easily be downloaded from the Internet or secured from the Bureau of Agricultural Research. Rather, my 20-minute spiel should, at the very least give them some very practical, commonsensical, user-friendly, value-added information, which I am sharing in this Linkages article now.

The first practical and strategic recommendation I gave was for the scientific community (government research facilities, the academic institutions, and the extension services) **to build, source, tap and use social networks that will link them to potential users** of such research and development outputs.

Just like us in the BSLBA, I told them to be a member of business associations or work to be invited to their meetings or tap friends in these networks so as to touch base with the business and industry people. By getting exposed to the business and industry people in less formal and academic situations and in the latter's own turf, the scientific community will case the business joints, so to speak, in a friendlier atmosphere. They will then get valuable information on how business people think, what they need, and what moves them.

The scientific community uses "method talk" - the working vocabulary and syntax of research procedures in the academe and in the research facilities. I finally understood and appreciated the strange world of "method talk" when I enrolled recently for my doctorate. The structure and the language of scientific inquiry demand a different vocabulary, a different syntax and dictate a different cadence. Hence, practically all research papers that are churned out of the two "production sites" of knowledge – the research institutions and the academe - are steeped in the highly technical vocabulary of quantitative positivism. Their papers are peppered with polysyllabic words; the sentences are long-winded; and since they have to laboriously build up theories, their works are substantiated by numerous tables and matrices. The research papers are oftentimes very voluminous.

"Method talk" sounds and looks complicated to a businessman or a corporate manager whose "*span of attention*" normally covers a one-page report. Oftentimes, in business, we do not have the luxury of time to cogitate and perorate. At most, we are three-pager fellows. With anything beyond three pages, we get impatient. Our minds are oftentimes processing several projects at the same time and we are ready to implement at any moment's notice and on parallel runs at that. We are not conditioned to read or listen to long reports.

Hence, my second recommendation for the promotion and adoption of R&D outputs was **to re-cast or re-package the research papers into compact market-driven technology transfer materials.**

This leads me to my third recommendation which was to ask the scientific community **to review their target markets for their promotional materials**. Right now, what I see is that there are two major markets for their researches. The research institutions and the academe are currently serving – (1) the scientific community itself and (2) the "stand-alone," individual farmers and the fishermen. They are hitting the two ends of their market continuum, but are missing out on the more organized businesses in agriculture and fisheries as well as the potential venture capitalists who straddle the space between the scientific community and the farmers and the fishermen.

Businessmen and venture capitalists as well as financing institutions are interested in technologies that would address two things: increase in productivity and decrease in cost of operations. The businessmen need not know the details of how the scientists arrive at their conclusions. They also need not learn the details of the "how to's" as in the case of the farmers and the fishermen. What they want to focus on are the feasibility and viability of the scientific findings and how these would affect the bottom line, the sustainability of operations, and the impact on their stakeholders.

It is, therefore, most strategic to hit the middle circle in the illustration above – the businessmen. And if this is so, there is still a need to re-cast or re-package the researches so that the promotional materials can be user-friendly for the businessmen. Hence, the second recommendation is very much contingent on how the scientific community views its market. The combination of recommendations No. 2 and No. 3 may in time even create a new path of relationships among the three markets, which may make communications among the three groups self-initiated rather than imposed or artificially initiated by government instrumentalities.

My fourth and last recommendation to the science community was **to keep their ears close to the ground.** There are really many things happening around and it just requires being aware and in the know of what is going on. This goes true for us as well, members of BLSBA. Then, of course, we should not stop at just keeping our ears on the ground. We have to seize the opportunities and become what is now known as a **"techno-entrepreneur."**

I recently attended the "1st National Conference on Entrepreneurship in Education" at the Ateneo De Manila University and learned that the DOST has the "Small Enterprises Technology Upgrading Program – DOST-Academe Enterprise Development Program" or known as "SETUP-DATBED". This program encourages turning what I call "hard core scientific outputs" into practical technologies for enterprise development.

In fact, there are about 95 reported projects housed in different academic institutions, majority of them startups that have been or are still being supported by this program. However, Dr. Teresita C. Fortuna, head of DOST NCR, lamented that there were not enough materials for new technologies. Much of what were being funded stand on old technologies.

Mr. Federico Gonzales, the executive director of the newly organized Philippine Center for Entrepreneurship, also spoke in the above conference.

PCE is a private sector-led initiative which believes that entrepreneurship can be a powerful agent of development. They have this very interesting project called - the Business Plan Competition which they have just recently launched under the acronym PESO (Philippine Emerging Startups Open). The competition addresses exactly what the scientific community wants (and which I think, we in the business sector also envisions to achieve) – promotion and adoption of the R&D outputs in business ventures. The program encourages the coming together of science and technology and champions from the business sector to come out with business plans using innovative ideas for enterprise development that will make money and contribute to the economic growth of the country.

A similar exercise was done in Dumaguete City, Negros Oriental recently whereby the Department of Trade and Industry and the local government, together with the Negros Oriental Business Development Foundation mounted the NOBDF Innovation Awards. Participants had to submit business plans which are standing on technology innovation platforms. The winners got cash prizes to start up their winning enterprise and obtained access to resources for team building, mentoring, education and capital, on the condition that the enterprise be based in Negros Oriental.

Five emerged as winners, namely: automated watering system, wireless alarm for cell phones, cost effective ink jet and photo copying ink, bricks from waste materials, and lastly, - the one I fell in love with – live fish transported without water.

This last project was done by a team of Silliman University graduates out of a masteral thesis done by Engr. Boni Comandante several years ago. His thesis, I believe, had to do with sex change of fish. I am not quite sure anymore, which is which and how, but one gender feeds a lot more than the other and that is why there was this proposition to do sex change in order to contain costs in feeding the fish. In any case, the procedure requires the fish to hibernate as the process of sex change was done in a solution that allows fish to sleep in an almost no-water environment.

Latching on to the idea of fish living in an almost no-water environment for a limited period of time, Engr. Comandante who took time off from his work in sales, and his team crafted a business plan based on transporting live fish without water. The project involves manufacturing of anti-stress salts that imitates a condition of hibernation. Based on experiments conducted, immersing the fish in a water bath containing a salt solution ensures 100% survival of fish within a nine-hour period. The fish jumps to life as soon as it is put in the water again.

As we all know, when we fly in live fish from Iloilo or Capiz to Manila, they need water to sustain them till they land. In fact, the greater part of the transport cost is for the space and weight eaten up by water. By introducing the SALT technology, the transport cost is said to be down by 75% because you don't have to carry as much water as before. And you can even pack a lot more fish this way.

This winning business plan will franchise the use of the technology via manuals and the training of handlers in the proper use of the technology. The

SALT solution itself will be sold separately by the franchisees. Both the anti-stress salt and the technology of transporting live fish without water are covered by applications for Philippine patent and copyright.

In any case, if I remember the story right, Mr. Boni Comandante whose technology was used for the project was so happy receiving his P50,000 cash prize on the night of the awarding and was about to leave the venue to celebrate, ready to resume his normal life in sales. Well, I believe he was called back. *"Young man, where do you think you are going? If you are interested to pursue the project, there is P4.0M capitalization waiting for you."*

And so, it seems Mr. Comandante is no longer into sales. He is now a **techno-entrepreneur** – successfully bridging the great divide between science and business. Isn't that inspiring? On that high note, I would like you to pick up from here and **be a techno-entrepreneur yourself**.

"Quality First": An Enterprise's Ultimate Challenge

Joel Amante

The success of a business is basically determined by the effectiveness of its management. Ultimately then the quality of people in management determines the success of a business. If a business is faltering or is less than what it was envisioned to be, the way the business is being run must be changed. But herein lies the challenge, the challenge of how to reinvent an organization and the challenge of how to change entrenched human behavior.

One of the great Japanese industrialists, Konosuke Matsushita, founder of Matsushita Electric Industries, said that one has to "make people first before making products." Matsushita firmly believed that only quality people can make quality products and services. Hence even before embarking on any change program, one has to first instill in people's minds the essential values required for achieving business excellence.

In the implementation of Total Quality Management or TQM, several core concepts need to be learned, practiced and integrated in the way work is done. The first of these concepts is the philosophy of "Quality First", not "quantity first" nor "cost first". The value of this concept can be seen in operations where the most economical way of making a product, for instance, is by producing only the exact quantity required by a customer. If there is no quality in designing a product, one has to make more than what is required to cover losses due to defects. Aside from doing more, rework often needs to be done as well that eventually results in higher costs. By considering quality first, therefore, one automatically creates the right quantity and the right cost at the same time.

Quality first requires that a quality attitude be adopted by everyone in an organization. It is said that the creation of anything of value consists of two steps: first is the conceptualization in the creator's mind and second is the actual physical creation. If there is quality in the way a product or service is conceived, there is a good likelihood that a quality product or service will be created. A quality mind conceives and creates quality processes which in turn will create quality products and services.

So the next time you hear "Pwede na yan" have it replaced by "Pwedeng Pwede." Let's change our culture of accepting second-rate products and services and always think of quality first even if sometimes, quantity or cost first seems more expedient.

Business Excellence: "Control at the Source"

Joel Amante

Frank Pryce in his book, "Right Every Time", wrote about the city of Hamburg in the late nineteenth century where the city fathers, faced with the problem of disposing of the city's human waste, built a sewerage system which discharged its contents into the river half a mile upstream of the city's fresh water supply uptake. In October 1890, over ten thousand Hamburg citizens perished from the poisoned river.

It is hard to imagine poisoning our own drinking water like what happened in the city of Hamburg but oftentimes, when we encounter customer complaints in our businesses, what we usually do is look at the downstream processes instead of the upper stream ones where the "poison" was most likely introduced. As one Japanese CEO puts it, "if clear water flows from the upper stream, there is no need to purify it farther downstream".

What is sometimes not so obvious to us is that the "poisoned" upper stream processes (marketing, research and development, planning and engineering) come about by default or by accident. Let me explain with an example. Drew, et al, in "Journey to Lean" wrote about an entrepreneur who sets up a small bakery at her home with only a mixing machine and an oven. As with most start-ups, she set up, by necessity, a fairly lean operating system that is flexible and that creates little waste without her realizing it.

Because this woman's bread is very good, the business begins to grow, and a few years later, the business develops into a medium-sized business with several locations, a variety of products, hundreds of employees and thousands of customers.

The business, however, has now become quite complicated. Once she used to plan in the afternoon for the next morning; now she relies on other people and an IT system to tell her what needs to be done. Before, she herself drove the one van she had; today she has a fleet of trucks that deliver fresh bread and other products to several outlets. Before, customers only needed to talk to her; now, resolving customer complaints has become a complex undertaking involving several people.

With a growing business like this, little thought is given to adding new capacity in a systematic and methodical way. In most cases, the configuration of assets, resources and people just happens; it is by accident rather than design. Before she knows it, what used to be an appropriate start-up system has now turned out to be inappropriate that results in numerous problems downstream: quality problems in products and services, cost overruns, operational errors, delayed deliveries, safety problems and a growing number of customer complaints.

What she also doesn't realize is that these downstream problems are created by upper stream processes that have become "poisoned" by default or by neglect. Not knowing any better, she applies quick fixes or "band-aid" solutions that immediately solve the problems but only to come back in a matter of days or weeks. In the meantime the stream of poisoned water continues to flow unabated.

Controlling at the source tells us that by focusing and working on the upper stream processes, downstream problems will be eliminated. For example, through thoughtful design, careful planning and adequate review of the product development process, raw material quality can be ensured, the right equipment can be procured, the appropriate measurement systems can be implemented and robust methods can be developed so that quality problems and operational errors are eliminated. Instituting an effective hiring process and an efficient training program can prevent poor employee performance that usually leads to delayed deliveries, numerous customer complaints and even safety problems. At times, even the design of the organizational structure itself needs to be reviewed and revised to prevent an overwhelmed entrepreneur from making hasty or incorrect decisions.

Solving problems downstream may temporarily ease the situation but the problems remain. One needs to look at the source of the problems and control these at the source. In more than half a century of quality management, the Japanese have learned that ninety percent of product or service quality is determined at the design phase, and that only ten percent of it is determined during production, inspection or service. Hence a lot of effort is expended upfront, at the upper stream processes instead of focusing efforts on problems downstream.

The lesson is clear: control at the source, do upper stream management.

Sale Options

Norman Golez, Llb

In our community where businesses abound, we cannot overlook the importance of a sale contract since it is the very reason each establishment thrives. Hence, awareness of our rights and remedies under the law becomes a must.

Oftentimes, sellers are faced with the dilemma in case a sale transaction does not proceed smoothly. Thus the question lies -- can the seller unilaterally rescind a contract of sale in the event that the buyer fails to pay the price? The answer is yes. It is important to note that "[t]he power to rescind obligations is implied in reciprocal obligations, in case one of the obligors should not comply with what is incumbent upon him." (Art. 1191, New Civil Code of the Philippines).

The law pertains particularly to reciprocal obligations. These are obligations wherein the two parties promise to do or give something to each other. It arises from the same cause and that the performance of one is conditioned upon the simultaneous fulfillment of the other (p. 175, Commentaries and Jurisprudence on the Civil Code of the Philippines, Vol. IV by Arturo Tolentino).

Interestingly, there may be instances wherein one of the parties is already willing and able to comply with his obligation while the other is not. In such an event, the law provides the injured party two (2) remedies: specific performance and rescission.

Specific performance compels the other party to comply with his obligation. This remedy always requires the intervention of the courts.

In the alternative, the injured party may ask for the rescission of the contract. Rescission is the cancellation of the contract or reciprocal obligation previously entered into by the parties. Notably, the power to rescind is granted to the injured party under Article 1191. It is predicated on the breach of faith by one party who violates his obligation to the other (Velarde v. Court of Appeals, 56 SCRA 361 [2001]). This right or power is implied in all reciprocal obligations and need not be expressly stipulated upon.

Rescission may be done with or without the intervention of the courts. Court intervention is not necessary when the object of the obligation has not yet been delivered. In such a case, mere declaration by the injured party of the cancellation of the obligation is sufficient.

However, if delivery was already made, judicial approval of the rescission is necessary to enable the party to recover what he has delivered. It should be noted that the right to rescind is not absolute. Verily, for rescission to be allowed by the courts, the breach must be so substantial and fundamental that it defeats the object of the parties of the obligation. Hence, slight or mere casual breach will not warrant the resolution of the obligation. (Ang vs. Court of Appeals, 170 SCRA 286 [1989]).

Significantly, in the event that both parties committed a breach of the obligation, the liability of the first infractor shall be equitably tempered by the courts.

However, if it cannot be determined which of the parties first violated the contract, the same shall be extinguished and each shall bear his own damages. (Article 1192, New Civil Code of the Philippines.)

SECTION SIX: BARANGAY INITIATIVES

A New Sunday Habit

Barangay San Lorenzo's Sunday Market @ Legazpi Car Park

Marlene Po

Independence Day 2005 was marked by Barangay San Lorenzo in an altogether unique way. With a cultural minority group providing the music and people milling around in Filipiniana garb, the "Sunday Market @ Legazpi Carpark" was launched, led by Chairman Joshua John Santiago. This early, it has been getting rave reviews because of the different products and activities being offered. For many, spending the whole morning at the market has become a Sunday habit.

As early as 7:00 am, one can choose from U.S. roast beef with mashed potatoes and delicately scrambled eggs, *sinangag* with various types of toppings, *bibingka* and *puto bumbong*, hot chocolate, crepes, or even *lechon* and roast calf. The tree-shaded car park houses more than 150 vendors in huge tents and at nine o'clock, the place is teeming with market goers trying specialties from Bataan, Quezon, Cavite, Cagayan de Oro, Bacolod and international dishes such as Indian, Cuban, Japanese, Thai, Spanish, Indonesian.

A dizzying array of pastries, cakes, cookies, *kakanin* entice the gourmands while for the figure-conscious, dairy products as well as fruits and vegetables – organic and otherwise – are available at competitive prices. There is also fresh seafood - to go or cooked on the spot *dampa*-style.

However, food is not the only attraction at the Sunday Market @ Legazpi Carpark.

To highlight the artistry of the Pinoy and to increase appreciation of our rich indigenous culture, the market now has an Arts and Crafts Section where one can find authentic jewelry, accessories and blouses from the T'Bolis - all handcrafted by students of the School of Indigenous Knowledge and Traditions in Lake Sebu, South Cotabato. There are also hand woven malongs from Magindanao; table runners, placemats and bags from the Yakan; antiques from the B'laan, Mandaya, Bagobo, Maranao; colorful mats from Samar; inlaid shell, bags from Bicol and so on.

Another facet of the Sunday Market @ Legazpi Carpark is its Outreach Program. Tables have been allotted to civic organizations and educational institutions with livelihood programs so the market can serve as an outlet for their products, such as the KILUS Foundation - which makes bags from recycled juice packs - and the T'boli School.

For the children, there are demo-workshops conducted by experts from the Education Division of the National Museum every first and third Sundays of the month. Activities include Casting and Molding, Clay Candle Holder Making, Mask Making & Painting, Paper Frame Making, Eggshell Mosaic, Silk Screening, Feathers as Décor, Mat Weaving, Storytelling, and so on.

This concept is a **first** in any market or bazaar and Barangay San Lorenzo is proud to have introduced this innovation. One shopper, whose child was so engrossed in her artistic task, enthused: "It's like a day care center in a market!" Yet another was so impressed that she finalized arrangements for the Museum facilitators to set up a kids' workshop in their upcoming bazaar.

Many exciting events have been lined up until the Christmas season, like street performances by gymnasts and mime artists; arnis and yoyo demonstrations; an On-the-Spot Painting competition organized by the National Museum. Some Sundays will feature specialties by province and foreign community. Grade schoolers will be invited to man their own booths – perhaps their first taste of entrepreneurship. Raffle promos in collaboration with Asian Spirit are in store for frequent shoppers. Major hotels within Barangay San Lorenzo will likewise be invited to present special spreads.

Thus, for the organizers – Ernie Moya, Carmina Ortega and Marlene Po – the work does not start and end on a Sunday. Because of the continuous effort to search for unique products and to find special attractions for the whole family - the Sunday Market @ Legazpi Carpark promises to be a multi-faceted Sunday habit for everybody.

There Is Hope Where There Is Discipline

Norman Golez

Imagine driving on a de-clogged thoroughfare in the heart of the Makati Central Business District at the peak of rush hour. Imagine crossing pristine streets and alleys, with no fears that your cellphone/bag might be snatched or that with each minute, your lungs are getting closer to heaven via lung cancer. Imagine spending Sunday with your family, searching for good pickings, lounging in the midst of trees and foliage, at the delightful Legaspi Park Organic Market. Imagine.

Barangay San Lorenzo, through the initiative of its Kagawad Atty. Norman T. Golez and under the potent leadership of Barangay Chairman Jay Santiago, has embarked on a new project which will make all these scenarios a reality.

This project, aptly named "TASK FORCE DISIPLINA", headed by Kagawad Atty. Golez, banks on the premise of (1) good city and barangay ordinances which benefit both the people and the government, (2) the strict and effective implementation of these ordinances as well as all relevant laws, and (3) the indispensable cooperation of its constituents. As they say, certain rights are tantamount to certain responsibilities.

Task Force Disiplina was launched on July 29, 2005 at the San Lorenzo Barangay Hall and was attended by representatives of various sectors such as the MAPA,

MAPSA, MACEA, Ayala Center Association, Ayala Land, Inc., Ayala Property Management Corporation and the San Lorenzo Village Association, among others.

Significantly, during the launch, the representatives of the various sectors expressed their willingness to become partners of Barangay San Lorenzo in transforming it into a model community characterized by a clean, disciplined and progressive citizenry. This willingness was formalized during Task Force Disiplina's subsequent meeting held on 10 August 2005 wherein its organizational structure was established.

To adequately prepare itself for its mission, Task Force Disiplina went through proper guidance and training under the tutelage of distinguished resource speakers in a three-day lecture series. On the first day of the lecture series, Task Force Disiplina was re-educated on the relevant Makati City and Barangay San Lorenzo Ordinances. On the second day, Task Force Disiplina was taught the Rights of the Accused and the proper arrest and seizure procedures. Finally, on the third day, the relevant provisions of the Revised Penal Code were taught to our law enforcers.

As aptly explained by its Head, Kagawad Atty. Golez, the ultimate goal of Task Force Disiplina is this: "Amidst all the economic and political turmoil facing the country today, many have started to lose hope. Task Force Disiplina aims to show that through discipline, there is still hope for the country. May pag-asa pa, basta may disiplina."

Ayala Land: Solid Waste Management

In its commitment to contribute to the preservation of the environment and provide efficient service to members, merchants and customers, Ayala Land's Ayala Malls Group, through the Ayala Center Association (ACA) continues to develop innovative ways in promoting the ecological solid waste management (SWM) in Glorietta and Greenbelt.

Ayala Center's SWM program has been running for a decade now, starting with the pilot implementation of polystyrene and plastic waste collection and recycling in 1996 through the collaborative efforts of Ayala Center Association, Ayala Foundation, Inc., Brgy. San Lorenzo and Polystyrene Packaging Council of the Phils.

Designed as a campaign to further reduce solid wastes that go to the landfill, the SWM program was launched among the estimated 1000 members and merchants of Ayala Center.

Among the activities conducted included a continuing series of orientation sessions on SWM, dissemination of circulars on the guidelines of waste segregation at source and disposal system, setting up of a compartmentalized depository or materials recovery facility (MRF), strict monitoring and spot checks of the solid wastes brought to the MRF and the publication of SWM practices by selected merchants.

To sustain 100% participation, Ayala Center integrated the policy of "no segregation, no collection" into the housekeeping guidelines of all members and merchants. In support of this, an annual orientation on SWM is held with the assistance of Ayala Property Management Corp. (APMC) and Ayala Foundation (AFI). Being the property management of the Ayala Malls Group, APMC plays a crucial role in the monitoring of compliance by all merchants. As incentive, certificates of recognition signed by ACA, AFI and DENR are awarded to complying tenants and merchants during the annual Earth Day celebration.

ACA's solid waste partner-contractor, Jaram Hauling Corp. is responsible for the management of ACA's MRF. Jaram also helps in the enforcement of proper waste segregation by refusing to accept unsorted wastes and by preparing monthly monitoring reports. Jaram has just completed establishing its own MRF/eco-center in San Mateo, Rizal. Jaram's MRF contains a segregation, consolidation and storage area for recyclables, vermi-composting for biodegradable materials and a small-scale wastewater treatment.

Through this partnership with Jaram, Ayala Center's SWM program has generated employment opportunities for at least 20 people assigned at Glorietta and Greenbelt MRF's. Jaram's MRF also hired at least 50 people doing further segregation and consolidation of recyclable materials. Clearly, the SWM program offers income-generating opportunities among other benefits to the environment and the recycling industry.

Results of the monitoring activities show that Ayala Center was able to reduce its residual waste by as much as 87% since it took in Jaram Hauling Corp. as a partner. Participation rate of merchants was recorded at 100% with a compliance rate of 80%.

To ensure sustainability of the Ayala Center's SWM program, a Technical Working Group (TWG) was formed, composed of Col. Wenceslao A Cruz and Ms. Lilia Sesperes of Ayala Center Association, Ms. Adel Licos of Ayala Foundation Inc, Engr. Erickberth Calupe of Ayala Property Management Corporation and Ms. Avella Lipata of Jaram Hauling Corporation. In addition to the continuous monitoring and information campaign activities, the TWG also spearheaded the drafting of the Ayala SWM manual that will serve as guide for the SWM program.

Ayala's SWM program has been a venue for learning by several interest groups, including local and international SWM training program participants, as well as the subject of case presentations in some local and international conferences on SWM. Its program has been gaining nationwide recognition with Ayala Foundation acclaimed as an Environmental Champion in the 5th edition of the World Bank's Philippine Environment Monitor.

Ayala Center's Materials Recycling Facility (MRF) was also cited as the first in the country that has been set up within a commercial center development. In addition, the Philippine Daily Inquirer featured Ayala as having the best waste management system in its June 27, 2005 issue.

Beep Revisited

Norman T. Golez

"An estimated 33,500 persons were reported dead while 114,000 were injured due to the strong earthquake that hit Metro Manila ..." This is a scenario that nobody wants to be a part of. A Japanese-funded study (Metro Manila Earthquake Impact Reduction Study) has revealed that great damage will be suffered from an earthquake in the West Valley Fault with a 7.2 magnitude.

While earthquakes are not avoidable, much less predictable, THERE IS NO EXCUSE FOR UNPREPAREDNESS. Accordingly, Barangay San Lorenzo has come up with a barangay-wide earthquake drill, otherwise known as, the Building Emergency Evacuation Plan ("BEEP") Project.

With the notable participation of building administrators/occupants, and the invaluable assistance of the Office of the City Mayor, the Office of Civil Defense and the National Disaster Coordinating Council, Philippine Institute of Volcanology and Seismology ("PHIVOLCS"), Makati Traffic Enforcement Unit, Ayala Center Association, Makati Commercial Estate Association, Makati Public Safety, Makati Parking Authority, Ayala Property Management Corporation, and the Makati Fire Department, Barangay San Lorenzo has launched its BEEP project.

The BEEP Project was divided into three distinct phases. The first phase began on November 2005 with a series of seminars conducted by the PHIVOLCS. Its main objectives were to educate the building administrators on the standard operating procedures during an earthquake and the critical elements in creating their own respective BEEP, which will be implemented and tested during the third phase of the project.

The second phase of the BEEP Project is the division and grouping into clusters of the approximately 300 buildings located within the Barangay. These clusters were organized in accordance with their strategic location and aggregate population.

Thereafter, each cluster elected their respective head. In order to avoid, or at least minimize, any casualty which may result from a stampede and to systematize crowd control during an earthquake or other similar emergency, each cluster was given a detailed evacuation route and a designated evacuation site. Thus, the location and lot area of available open spaces within the Barangay were also identified and matched with each cluster during this phase.

The third and final phase of the project involved the implementation of the various buildings' BEEPs. Actual building evacuation drills were done per cluster or group of clusters, twice weekly from June to July 2006. In connection with these drills, Barangay San Lorenzo organized various teams, specifically, Evacuation, Site Security, Fire-Safety, First Aid, Communications, and Search and Rescue. On the part of the building administrators, they echoed and imparted to the buildings' occupants what they learned during the first phase of the BEEP Project. Particular focus was given to the "Duck, Cover and Hold" exercise, possible earthquake hazards, proper care and assistance of persons with disabilities and the conduct of a Head Count at the evacuation site.

An evaluation of the BEEP project's groundwork reveals that a more aggressive educational campaign must be pursued. Although majority of the building occupants did participate, a qualitative assessment of the said participants' attitude indicates apathy and indifference. Clearly, the gravity of the situation is yet to be recognized by the Barangay's populace. Moreover, numerous buildings that participated did not have properly functioning emergency light fixtures and alarm systems. Other material issues were also identified, i.e. insufficiency of open spaces, lack of proper communication equipment, and the lack of a Mass Casualty Incidence Command System.

To address these inadequacies, Barangay San Lorenzo has stepped up its efforts in improving the Barangay's disaster preparedness. Future actions shall include the enactment of an ordinance that will enjoin all building administrators to implement their BEEP and conduct an annual drill. Further, training on Mass Casualty Incidence Command System procedures will begin in the last quarter of 2006.

Nobody wants to be part of the "33,500 dead, 114,000 injured" scenario. The groundwork has been laid. However, to rise above the ground entails the concerted efforts and cooperation between Barangay San Lorenzo and the other relevant government offices.

Know Your Ka-Barangay

Kath del Rosario

A. Name: **RAMONA HABANA**
Position: Barangay Nurse
Responsibilities: Disseminates health information; assists the Barangay doctors.

Our clinic-goers certainly find her warm smile comforting. Tita Mona to others, she started working with us on March 5, 2005. She takes charge of coordinating and facilitating our health and sanitation projects within the Barangay.

A nursing graduate of the last exclusive batch of La Concordia College in 1983 under the management of Daughters of Charity, she spent her internship at Cardinal Santos Memorial Hospital. She has extensive working experience as staff nurse, intensive care unit nurse and emergency room nurse.

"I cannot forget the values I learned from my nun supervisors during my college days. That is why being of service to my countrymen is always in my heart," Tita Mona said.

She describes herself as a person who gets emotionally affected by the suffering of her patients. Residents as well as other co-employees describe Nurse Ramona as a professional, caring and disciplined nurse who always follows the rules set in the Barangay Clinic.

B. Name: **MARILYN KING**

Position: Lupon Secretary II
Responsibilities:
1.   In-charge of the issuance of Constituents'
Barangay ID (identification cards);
2.   Receives constituents' formal complaints,
barangay cases, and blotters;
3.   Assists in handling inquiries.

Marilyn started as a clerk in Barangay San Lorenzo in
January 1994. In 1999, she was assigned as
bookkeeper.

When Brgy. Capt. Santiago took over; she was
designated as Community Affairs Assistant II. She is
now Lupon Secretary II.

"Siguro nagtagal ako rito kasi masyado akong friendly.
Marami akong kaibigan dito. Ultimong mga residente,
househelpers and drivers kilala ako."

"To keep one's job," Marilyn said, "one must be
hardworking and honest."

"Ang nais ko ay ma aksyonan agad ano man ang
kailangan ng constituent." She has been in the service
for almost 13 years.

When asked what she can say about Brgy. San
Lorenzo, "Talagang napamahal na sa akin ang
barangay na ito dahil sa tagal ng paninilbihan ko dito."

C. Name: **ERIC PAULE**
Position: Barangay Inspector

This 30-year old barangay inspector may be a man of few words but not during work.

His position needs a lot of legwork where he does the inspection of construction sites to check permits, fire exits, electrical layouts and more.

"Pag walang permit at nagko-construct automatic may penalty yun," he quips.

He also does the rounds of checking business permits in all business establishments in Barangay San Lorenzo.

Already two years in the service, Eric is an architectural graduate of Technological University of the Philippines (TUP).

Milenyo Aftermath

Ernie Moya

MOTHER NATURE DEFINITELY COMMANDS A
LOT OF RESPECT. This thought was inescapable for
those of us who helplessly watched as Typhoon
Milenyo unleashed its fury around midday of
Thursday, the 28th of September 2006. Who could
forget the feeling of being put on edge as rain and
winds uprooted trees, knocked down electric poles and
sent debris flying all over? We certainly feared for our
lives in anticipation of a roof, walls or any type of
contraption collapsing on us. Fate dictates as to who
would incur loss or damage, thereby affirming the
meaning of the term force majeure.

Inside San Lorenzo Village, the overall damage was
phenomenal. One long-time resident remarked that he
has never seen such widespread damage in decades.
An assessment of the destruction showed that all
except two streets were made impassable by fallen
vegetation and debris.

A total of twenty-five big trees were uprooted. Five of
these were considered landmark as they were
practically as old as the village and presumed to be
invulnerable enough to outlive us all. Eight Meralco
posts either leaned or fell, and some power lines were
destroyed thus causing electric disruption throughout.
For some residents, it took as long as a week for
electric service to be restored. Two parked vehicles
were crushed, while several houses incurred either
minor or major damages.

Capt. Santiago and the Barangay Council promptly formed a clearing task force composed of Barangay employees and volunteers mostly from Botanical Garden. Emergency purchases of additional tools and gadgets were made. Aside from JARAM, our garbage contractor, the services of other hauling and trucking firms were mobilized.

As a result, almost all streets were partially cleared and made accessible to vehicles within twelve hours. By Saturday, major thoroughfares such as San Lorenzo Drive, Ponce, Joaquin, Juan Luna and Amorsolo Streets were almost totally cleared.

Community spirit and perseverance prevailed as the employees and volunteers gave their all to get the job done.

540 Benefit from SanLo's Learn-to-Earn Program

Gino Bolos

A total of seventeen livelihood and skills training programs were conducted by Barangay San Lorenzo under its Learn-to-Earn Program, during the last quarter of 2005 and January 2006, benefiting some 540 participants who are mostly constituents of the barangay, out-of-school-youth and unemployed.

According to Barangay San Lorenzo Chairman Joshua John Santiago, the program is designed to empower participants with the right training and knowledge in their chosen field of interest. He also said that the barangay is teaming up with BSLBA to assist the graduates for possible on-the-job training and later regular employment, or entrepreneurship if they want to set up their own businesses.

The training modules conducted were: Computer Literacy Course, Computer Repair, Cellular Phone Technician Course, Reflexology, Refrigeration and Airconditioning, Clowning, Cosmetology, Tailoring, Dressmaking, Beadworks, Waitering and Bartending, Baking and Meat Processing. A crash course on Computer Secretarial was also conducted.

Barangay San Lorenzo Council Approves Construction of Sewage Facility

Ernie Moya

After evaluating the long-term benefits and with an assurance that all technical safeguards are in place, the Barangay San Lorenzo Council passed a resolution approving the construction of a sewage flow balancing facility by Manila Water.

The project is a totally enclosed underground holding tank to collect and store excess sewage flow during peak periods. When the volume of sewer flow is at the minimum, the sewage in the holding tank will be pumped into the sewer trunk main. The site selected is an Ayala-owned 1,050-square meter parking lot located at the corner of de la Rosa and Amorsolo Streets in Barangay San Lorenzo. With an estimated cost of Php 40 million and a capacity of 5,000 cubic meters/day, the project will ensure continuous treatment efficiency and allow further expansion of sewer services in the busy area consisting of Makati Central Business District (CBD) and the surrounding villages.

The Makati City sewerage system was built in 1964. The said sewerage system collects and treats sewage flows largely from the Makati Central Business District (MCBD). It issues the activated sludge treatment technology and is designed with a maximum capacity of 40 million liters per day (MLD).

Recent measurements indicate that flows into the STP peak at 39 MLD level. The increase in flows resulted largely from the rehabilitation and upgrading works in the sewer network in 1999 and the continuous development of the CBD.

The situation is of concern because Makati sewage flows are expected to increase over time. From 1997 to 2005, wastewater treated at the Makati STP increased from an average daily flow of 20 MLD to 35 MLD. The proposed project will address this increase in demand through mechanisms for regulating flows into the system while allowing for further sewerage service expansion.

Another related issue is the increased detention of the sewage in the system. This changes the flow regime, resulting in the slower full-pipe flow which increases the potential of the solids to settle in the pipes and manholes. This can lead to increased septicity and hydrogen sulfide associated with foul odors and accelerated corrosion of the system.

The provision of a flow balancing facility to provide controlled storage of excess flow during the high flow periods was found to be the most feasible option to mitigate the risks in the system. It is considered that the installation of a well-located underground holding tank would lead to the reduction of septicity within the system and lessen the risk of wastewater flows to the street.

Population Survey

Ernie Moya

AVAILABILITY OF RELIABLE STATISTICS is indeed vital to effective planning. At the Barangay level, information on population is crucial in assessing priority issues and needs. It provides a roadmap by which policy makers can employ limited and scarce resources in organizing an efficient and sustainable development plan.

Here in Barangay San Lorenzo, our official population record dates as far back as the year 2000. This also coincides with the last NSO official census. With the rapidly changing times, this database borders on inadequacy and obsolescence. Hence, updating and computerizing this information is our urgent and compelling need.

To address such urgency, our Barangay Council enacted Barangay Ordinance No. 002 Series of 2006 which is an affirmation of Section 394 d (6) of the Local Government Code and similar governmental regulations such as DILG Memorandum Circular 2001-032 and Section 7 of Presidential Decree 651. All these effectively mandate that a record be kept and regularly updated on all inhabitants of each barangay to contain the following information: name, address, place and date of birth, sex, civil status, citizenship, occupation and such other information as may be prescribed by law or ordinance.

To implement this Ordinance, our Barangay is conducting a survey among its households. Inside San

Lorenzo Village, the valuable assistance of Assumption College was solicited. The school administration agreed to adopt the activity as the school's community outreach project. Student volunteers from the collegiate level were appointed as survey takers or "enumerators". As expected, these students are able to rally support from the villagers. Their participation enhances the integrity and trustworthiness of the endeavor.

In Legazpi Village, the assistance and cooperation of the building administrators/owners were likewise sought. The building administrators themselves or their assigned personnel were tasked to conduct the survey within their respective buildings.

Prior to actual field operations, the student volunteers and building administrators attended an orientation workshop conducted by the National Statistics Office (NSO). They were familiarized with the survey form and how to collect complete and accurate information. They were also taught how to systematically enumerate households within their assigned zones.

Some may argue that this exercise is an infringement on privacy. However, it is also the Barangay's duty to comply with rules and laws governing it. Having the right population information is indeed very vital to governance. How, for instance, can the cost of a project be justified without identifying the size of its target beneficiaries? How can the barangay spread benefits when the rightful stakeholders do not come forward and register with the Barangay?

Clearly, an accurate and reliable population database is essential for the following reasons:

---- as a guide for city planners in mapping out development strategies based on demographic considerations. The City of Makati is formulating a city-wide medium- to long- term plan called "Makati 21" with reference to the 21st Century. All Makati barangays are thus relied upon to provide trustworthy demographic input for this undertaking.

---- as an identity landmark for residents for the issuance of clearances and for entitlements to benefits. Benefiting from Barangay-sponsored programs and projects is a privilege reserved first and foremost for Barangay constituents. Anyone who wishes to avail of these should register with our Barangay.

---- as a means to justify budget allocation for facilities and services directed at specific community sectors or stakeholders. A program or project can only be aptly justified by identifying and assessing the size of target beneficiaries which can be derived from the population database.

SECTION SEVEN: PERSONAL DEVELOPMENT

Do You Have a Wealthy Mind?

Dero Pedero

Why is it that one man can build a skyscraper while another can't even build a hut? Why can people like the Waltons of Walmart and Henry Sy of SM build and operate an impressive chain of malls and department stores while others couldn't even set up a sari-sari or convenience store?

Anyone can be rich but not everyone will be. Some people generate great wealth, while others don't because not everyone is capable of turning his wealth dreams and desires into reality.

What kind of a man creates great wealth? He is one of a very rare breed of humans—the super fortunate ones powered by a healthy mind.

QUALITIES OF A WEALTHY MIND

The greatest news you'll ever hear is that the wealthy mind can be developed. Any mind can be programmed for wealth and prosperity. This is why developing your money-making knowledge and skills—getting the right education, having the proper beliefs and attitudes, being in the right circle of friends and associates, and taking courses and seminars that boost your aptitude for wealthy-building--- is very important.

Is your mind programmed and geared for great wealth? Do you possess a wealthy mind? Find out if yours has these qualities:

The wealthy mind believes in the abundance of the universe. It is aware of the unlimited possibilities that exist, and chooses to unravel, solve, and exploit their mystery.

The wealthy mind dreams. It is not content with what there is, it formulates a vision of what could or should be.

The wealthy mind believes in the power of dreams and desires. It knows that it is God's co-creator. The wealthy mind has great faith in the Divine Providence but realizes that God only helps those who make things happen.

The wealthy mind creates. The wealthy mind is always improving, innovating, perfecting. It always looks for a better, more efficient, and more extraordinary way of doing things.

The wealthy mind has a purpose. There is a noble reason that rules over and above what it does that inspires and motivates it to imagine, create and set energy into motion.

The wealthy mind is clear and focused. It knows precisely what it wants and is not easily distracted by external disturbances.

The wealthy mind is courageous. Fear is not in its vocabulary because fear results in inaction, which produces nothing. It is neither afraid to take calculated risks nor afraid to lose it all.

The wealthy mind is persistent. It learns from its mistakes and keeps on trying until is succeeds.

The wealthy mind builds powerful alliances with others to attain great goals. It knows that with the synergistic help of the right people, it can achieve the impossible.

The wealthy mind loves what it is doing. It is passionate about its concepts and projects. Most of all, it knows how to enjoy and savor the fruits and benefits of its labors and creations.

The wealthy mind shares and gives. It does not believe in lack, it is generous and benevolent. The wealthy mind knows that the more it gives, the more it has, and the more it receives.

The wealthy mind knows that money is a means, not an end. It is aware that money is simply a tool to improve the condition of mankind.

Money is a Mind Thing

Here is one curious theory that I point out in my "Money, Money! Secret Principles of Money & Prosperity" seminars: If all the money in the world were gathered and distributed equally among all the people on earth, in three years, the rich would be richer and the poor would be poorer and even more miserable.

Money is truly a mind thing. You have to be wealthy in mind to be wealthy in money.

Lessons from the Pacman

Veredigno Atienza

The tributes keep pouring in for this humble provinciano from General Santos City with a limited education, an insignificant work background, no awe-inspiring pedigree, no political connections up to a few years ago, and no balance sheet that banks would have been interested in up to a few years ago.

Neither does he possess matinee idol looks nor does he seem to be a debutante's dream escort. He has an atrocious fashion sense: a perfect opportunity for "A Queer Eye for the Straight Guy." He speaks simply – no eloquence, no bravado, no scintillating wit, and no profound earth-shaking statements.

Despite all these shortcomings and disadvantages, Manny "The Pacman" Pacquiao has captured every Filipino's heart. For one brief shining moment he succeeded in uniting the country when he battled and defeated Mexico's Eric "El Terrible" Morales, a three-time world champion and considered a national treasure in his country.

Manny's phenomenal success and potential are truly mind-boggling. Some say he could even be our president someday. When he will become our president and how his presidency will look like – I will leave these to the experts.

These experts are the people who control the levers of power in our country, or at least who believe they do even if they actually don't, or those who believe they know the people who do, or who have been there and done that as far as power goes, or who will never know what power is but think they know all about it.

Let us stick to the simpler things. Let us look at Manny Pacquiao as he is right now and learn some valuable lessons that this man with inauspicious beginnings can teach each one of us.

First of all, this writer is taken in by his humility and simplicity. Walang yabang (none yet, so far so good). No airs. Simply down to earth. What you see is what you get. Every bit like a gust of fresh air in a smoke-filled room. His body language, the tilt of his head, his relaxed shoulders, his direct but gentle gaze, his steady gait, his language, his tone of voice, his message, they all convey simplicity and humility.

Second, his deep and abiding faith. He comes across like a little child in his Father's hands. He personifies faith. His job can snuff the life of anybody, including his, in a split second, and he is aware of this. He comes across as a man who has surrendered himself to God. Is this possible, that a man should totally be in the presence of God as he batters the face of his opponent? Yes, if he is like a sword in the hands of a swordsman.

Third, his complete professionalism. He trained longer and in a more focused manner than before for his fight against Eric Morales. While he is not considered a classic technical boxer like Morales, while he comes across as a brawler and street fighter, he takes and follows professional advice. He dedicates himself to become a better, more effective and more exciting boxer who is worth every cent paid by the viewing and paying public.

Fourth, his humane and kind heart. While he is a fighter through and through, he never forgets that boxing is just a job, and that Morales or any other opponent is not an enemy, but a colleague in the field of sports entertainment. He views the other guy as somebody exactly like him who just wants a better future for his family.

When he was asked what he prayed to God about before his flight with Morales, he said that he asked God to help him and to ensure that neither he nor his opponent Morales gets hurt.

Fifth, his basic sense of humor. When he was asked about his wife's advice prior to the Morales fight, Manny said:"She said: dalawang bagay lang yan: una kaliwa, pangalawa, kanan."

In one interview, his TV host forgot the title of the Philippine national anthem. Manny said "Dahil Sa Iyo". The TV host said "Papaano yon?" to which Manny replied "Di ba ang last line ng Anthem ay 'Ang mamatay ng dahil sa iyo?'"

Sixth, his unquestionable patriotism. His song says it all: "Para sa iyo ang laban na ito." He offers every fight, every blow he takes, and every punch he throws, for the Philippines and his countrymen, for their happiness, for their glory, for their unity. In his recent bout with Eric Morales, his overriding objective and sincere concern was to unite the Filipinos, to get them to understand and accommodate each other, "upang magkaintindihan na sana tayo."

Seventh, his raw courage. Ninoy Aquino once observed that if there is any one trait that Filipinos admire, it is courage. In his previous fight against Morales, Manny demonstrated his raw courage thru the blood streaming down his face for a good portion of the fight. He had the excuse to quit, a head butt, but he finished the fight, losing on points, a fight many believed he had won.

Eighth, his filial piety. At the ABS-CBN Magandang Umaga Bayan show, Manny appeared with his estranged parents. His parents are separated, and his father is now living with the other family. Manny demonstrated as much affection and respect for his father as he showed his mother. He seemed so happy just to see them together, just to be with them together.

He praised them both, whatever their differences may have been with each other, and for the manner he was raised. He thanked them profusely for their love, sacrifices, and advice. And he was so happy to tell the TV hosts and crew that he will bring his parents around for a shopping spree to buy anything to their heart's content.

In this land of ours, which is a valley of tears for many poor Filipino families, Manny expressed the eagerness to give his parents a taste of comfort and luxury that they never had before, and could never have, if not for their courageous and generous son Manny.

A Working Mother's Letter to Her Children

Kuku Lopez

Thank you for the flowers. Thank you for remembering me on this special day for mothers. As I look at all of you with your impish smiles, I feel a little sad knowing I am losing you guys faster than a blink. And I wish I could hold on to Time a little longer so I can enjoy you a little bit more. But I guess that is asking for the moon, you are all young men now ready to craft your own independent lives - so all I can hope for is that I have the composure to let you go with grace.

In many ways I am glad there is such a day as Mother's Day. It gives me special reason to write you this thank-you letter. It allows me to sit still and put down on paper how I feel about all of you. Sure, I say 'I love you' a lot and I hug and I kiss you a lot, earning the moniker "Kissing Monster." But I guess it is different putting down on paper my thoughts about you. Writing makes this whole experience of focusing just on you very, very special. Because as I write this letter, it is just you I am thinking about.

I remember telling your father some years back that you were all meant to be ours. As you have heard the story, there was a time I was really very, very frail and I kept on losing my babies. And, of course, you know how much I love babies. I promised God that I would be the best mother ever if He chose to give me one. I got the four of you so He must have been listening to me intently. And since a promise is a promise, I have made sure I remain the best mother ever to all of you.

And hey, thanks guys. You have been such a balm every time I felt low and sad and alone, especially on those times when your father's work brought him to far-away places. Your sidling up, twirling my hair, massaging my feet, preparing lovely meals, cracking funny jokes and being plain irreverent - make me feel so loved and so wanted - what else could a mother ask for? And thanks too for keeping me company every time your father is away. I do get scared being alone at night and your presence shoos my nightmares away. Mothers do get nightmares too!!! We don't really grow out of these juvenile things. We just learn to keep them to ourselves.

But there are certain things we can't keep to ourselves – our sermons. Mommies are always thought of by their kids as nags. Maybe we are. I think I am, though I tried very hard not to be one. But I guess we will not be good moms if we are not so. And I have a perfect explanation for that.

Like clay that one wants to form into a well-crafted vase, a person needs to be rolled, dabbed, flattened, stretched and softly patted for him to become a well-crafted human being. Most often, though not always, we, the moms are the potters. Until the moms feel their products have taken the form that we think could stand the test of time, we continuously subject our clay to the rolling and the stretching and the patting. Unfortunately, some parents take the process of crafting their creation literally – physically and psychologically battering their kids.

But many of us practice the craft in the most loving way we know how – by constantly talking and gabbing (which you call nagging) and hugging and loving our creations. We truly love and treasure our creations – never mind if our creations think of us as monsters and meddlers and pests.

Well, beloved irreverent bunch, I suppose you oftentimes feel you have been over-rolled and over-stretched and over-patted by my constant intrusions into your life. If there is one thing you have to know about potters, potters are usually determined creatures. Until they feel safely confident that their creations are what **ought to be** (of course, what ought to be is defined mostly by us based on our perceptions and our own formation) - **forming** goes on. So… what am I saying? Well, I guess it means I'll be on your case for a much longer time yet!!!

The first great pain a mother has is when she feels her child is no longer in need of her. It is such a paradox really! We train you from the time you come out of our wombs to learn to be independent and yet when you start being independent we hurt so much. So you see, my dear sons, mothers can be a pain in the *you-know-what*.

And since you are now my captive audience, I might as well play my role to the hilt and be a *you-know-what* some more. I told you – potters are determined creatures!!!! So here are some more nuggets to remember from the Queen Nag.

LEARN TO HAVE A GOOD LIFE

A good life doesn't always mean we have to have material things. A good life is not always about being rich or having things. A good life is knowing the value of what you have no matter how little it is. Being simple allows you less pressure in life and more time to enjoy life. And that is what we should be doing, enjoying life - enjoying relationships, laughter, good stories, blue skies, a good cry, hugging, etc. Do not make a mistake running after material things and having them as the measures of success. Otherwise, you will die of heart attack from the pressures of keeping up, of running after objects - and they are just that after all - only objects!! So why die for objects. If you have to die for something, die for principles, for something noble.

LEARN TO RISK

You also must remember that one gets hurt somehow no matter. Therefore, we cannot forever run away from risks or painful things. What we need to learn is how to get over the hurts or the fears. You must learn how to fight adversities - whether the fight is a physical fight or an emotional fight or a political fight. You have to have **courage**. You have to learn to risk. You cannot forever hide or run away. You must start facing and confronting your fears. Arm yourself with tools to fight. If knowing taekwondo gives you courage, then do take it up. If repeating a hurtful or a fearful experience will cure your pain or your fear, then repeat it. But do not keep on running or hiding.

LEARN GENTILITY

Please be gentler in your speech and manner; be less curt. Your curtness can be mistaken for snootiness or for impoliteness or for being brusque. Let them see the naughtiness, let them see the twinkle in your eyes; let them see how human you are but most of all let them see how gentle your souls are. Let this gentleness come out in your manner of speaking and comportment. I must say you are all now less 'pikon' but there is still some lurking in there. When you are, you become less amiable and you become more sarcastic and then the leprechaun character, which is so loveable in all of you, gets lost.

LEARN TO BE SPIRITUAL

We may not have given you the best examples in showing that life must also be lived spiritually. But I strongly believe there is a Supreme Being we have to thank for - for all the blessings we are getting. Both your father and I truly believe that there is God and while we may not have been religious in attending rituals it does not mean that we do not believe in the tenets of the Lord. We believe that we should not be intentionally malicious and vicious to our fellowmen. We believe in doing things the **right** way, the **just** way, the **charitable** way. We believe in caring for our fellowmen.

LEARN FROM YOUR ELDERS

There will be many more trials in your life. Be ready for them. Learn from us - your elders. Pick the worst of what you see in us and get lessons from them. Ask yourself why these "*not-so-nice-*

things" about your parents should not be emulated at all by you. **But - take the best of what we are and make them part of you**.

So there, beloved leprechauns, please accept my version of thanking you for remembering me on this Mother's Day. Truly, the flowers are lovely and they smell so nice.

SECTION EIGHT: TAXATION AND PUBLIC FINANCE

Getting the Toxin Out of Taxes

Veredigno P. Atienza

Taxes are like snake venom: they can kill, but they can also heal. When they are unreasonable, unfair, abusive, oppressive, confiscatory, predatory, when they make business uncompetitive with regard to costs, when they kill the sources of growth and sap the roots of our creativity and strength, when they do not go to government coffers or are outright stolen, then taxes are toxic.

When taxes are reasonable, when they allow businesses to compete among themselves and in the global market, when they leave enough in the wallet of the wage earner for a decent living, and in the purse of the consumer to boost the domestic market, when they are administered so as to allow business to survive and employ unutilized labor, when they provide services and employment, then taxes are positive and constructive.

The public has a natural aversion to taxes, tax collection and other forms of government collection: customs duties, toll fees, SSS / GSIS premiums, concession fees, and fund contributions, among others.

It is not unreasonable to expect the above natural reaction from the public. Since time immemorial, tax collection, whether done for datus, Spanish friars or Roman emperors, has never been popular.

Does this mean that we should not try to make taxes more palatable and more positive and constructive?

Obviously we should try, since taxes are such an integral part of our lives. Taxes are totally inevitable and so important, such that their collection cannot be left alone to the government. It is therefore necessary to package taxes in a more palatable, positive and constructive manner.

Where and how do we begin? The best way is thru information and education. The public has to learn more about government and public finance, how the government taxes every citizen, and how it spends Juan dela Cruz's hard-earned money.

There must be continuous information campaigns not just through the broadcast and print media, but perhaps most important, thru local schools, thru community organizations, public gatherings and every available opportunity.

The public should be educated on tax matters so that they would be equipped in understanding the issues at hand. Distrust has many roots, and among them are bad experience and ignorance.

With bad experience, there is nothing we can do except to prevent a repeat. On the other hand, correcting ignorance will in turn lead to better understanding and greater trust and cooperation between the government and the governed.

Increased public knowledge, vigilance and cooperation can make taxes more palatable, positive, constructive, and less toxic.

Misusing VAT

Dean O. de la Paz

At first they said that we were in a fiscal crisis. We believed them even when our economists debunked the term. In less than two months they said that we were out of it. We believed them again even when it takes as much as ninety days for an economic cycle to complete itself and at least two successive periods or 180 days to determine fiscal levels.

In order to fill the crisis level gaps that no longer existed in the proportions they said it did, they asked us to give them more money. That, after historic wanton spending for electoral legitimacy and a program of uncontrolled borrowings. Our gullibility seems to have no bounds. We believed them again and in Congress, we asked how much we should be giving, in what form and when.

They told us that it would be through the E-vat that now included economic producers such as power and oil companies. So that the empty coffers might again be filled, they threw in a conditional 2% additive.

To be true to the nature of a value added pass-on tax, E-vat impacts not on income generating taxpayers but on consumers. It is a pass-on tax, applied on sales and paid ultimately at the consumer end whether that consumer is an income generator or not. As such, it is applied where there is least resistance.

For some however, as the tax is applied at the upper end of a production chain, as it is on power and utilities where the inputs (energy, fuel and water) are simply raw materials and part of almost any product, the tax then turns exponential. Senator Pimentel questioned the constitutionality and Sen. Roxas had reservations on its application at the topmost portion of a productive chain where it wreaks the most havoc.

An analysis of our typical electricity bill however, proves both gentlemen are right when we unbundled our electricity bill and identified where the VAT is not only misapplied but by its mere presence inflicts an economic injustice.

One VAT application anomaly seems to be where consumers shoulder the franchise tax burdens of distribution utilities. Utilities are awarded franchises and for those they are taxed. However, as utilities append this franchise tax on their invoices, though a common practice, the consumer, in effect, is taxed the franchise liability. Now that is an anomaly.

It is, however, aggravated by the E-VAT. To apply a consumption tax on passed-on franchise taxes as does the E-Vat, effectively collects a non-consumption franchise tax from consumers. It seems energy authorities miscomprehended VAT. It is to be applied on the value of an input and not on just any cost component.

Another aberration on the misuse of the VAT is its application on systems loss where we seem to be paying a tax of 6.52% on systems loss changes.

Systems loss is the electricity lost from pilferage or technical and administrative ineptitude. Passed on to consumers, they are neither raw material nor input costs. They are spawned by inefficiencies and are by no means consumed.

Again here is a misapplication of the E-Vat. By taxing systems loss at the consumer level is double taxation for an anomaly suffered through electricity paid for but is neither received nor enjoyed. Neither cost inputs nor raw materials nor sales, inefficiencies are hardly input upon which a VAT should be applied.

Another unbundled item slapped an E-Vat is the Php 0.1125/kwh donated by consumers as a subsidy to others whose consumption allows them discounts ranging from 20% to 50%. Here applying E-Vat makes the least sense as the consumer is penalized for helping correct an economic imbalance. The donation is charged a VAT even as "lifeline rate" subsidies are neither inputs nor consumable by the entity paying the E-Vat.

Finally, an item worsened by Vat misapplications is the Currency Exchange Rate Adjustment (CERA) in our electricity bill. Why is VAT imposed on currency devaluations that it should be taxed?

At the end of the day it is not surprising that the public feels energy officials have been lying about the effects of E-Vat. On the eve of an additional 2% VAT, they again claim VAT will have little incremental effect. Unfortunately, for a public already at the cliff's edge, a tax misapplied, whether its effect is in the millions or simply a centavo, is one tax too expensive.

Know Your Tax Remedies

Jack Wong

It is the inherent power of the government acting through its legislature to impose a proportionate burden upon persons, property rights or transactions; so as to raise revenue to support its expenditure and as a tool for general and economic welfare.

There is a presumption that taxpayers file their taxes correctly in good faith and regularities. It is also presumed that there is non entitlement to tax deductions or tax refund or tax credit. Otherwise, the taxpayer will be subject to audit.

Taxpayer's rights and remedies

The taxpayer has the legal right to eliminate or reduce his tax liability as long as he does it through lawful means. If the taxpayer discovered lately that there was an erroneously filed return, he can immediately file an amended tax return within 3 years from the date of filing the original return provided that no audit notice has been received yet from BIR. So you only pay for the 20% deficiency interest due on unpaid amount without paying for the 25% surcharge.

If one does not have enough money to pay his tax due, he can request for an extension from BIR and pay his tax; at least he saves from paying surcharges, and he only pays for the tax liability plus the deficiency interest arising from the late payment.

Avoid non-filing of tax return; BIR will impose both deficiency interest plus the tax due with surcharges.

It's better to pay on time or late rather than not pay at all.

Auditing of Records and Books of Accounts

The revenue officers have the right to examine a taxpayer's books and records when the Commissioner gives them the go-signal to audit on a particular taxable year. They will examine books of accounts such as the general ledger, general journal, subsidiary ledgers and special journals. They also check invoices and receipts, journal vouchers, delivery receipts and reconciliation statements. They obtain information from third parties such as verifying your sales through records of your clients or reconciling your purchases with books of your suppliers. These will be used as basis for their assessment in case of tax deficiencies.

There are cases wherein the investigation process includes conducting inventory, stock-taking and on-site surveillance of the establishment through a mission order.

A tax audit can be conducted through LA (Letter of Authority) or TVN (Tax Verification Notice) or no-contact audit through letter notice. LA must be served within 30 days from the time it was issued and signed and must be finished within 120 days unless the taxpayer signs a Waiver of Statute of Limitations, thereby extending the validity of the LA.

General Rule: NO LA, NO AUDIT

Except in certain cases:
-non issuance of invoices
-unregistered books, invoices / receipts

-unpaid or illicit articles subject to excise tax

A BIR "White Paper" (informal invitation letter) is generally prohibited.

To avoid double or multiple issuances of LAs, write BIR a letter informing them of a previous LA with attached income tax return to it. In case of conflict between two LAs, ask a formal letter from the commissioner as to which revenue officer shall conduct the tax audit.

Usually, an LA signed by a higher national official prevails. It is dangerous to settle or finalize a tax case with a lower-ranked tax officer where another LA was issued by a higher-ranking tax official.

It is advisable to call the audit office to verify the genuineness of LA and examiners are mandated to show to the taxpayer their BIR identification cards when requested.

The taxpayer must write a letter of protest as to what selection criteria were the basis for audit procedure, then the regional officer will send a notice of informal conference with the taxpayer for procedural due process. Then the tax officer will prepare a report which states whether or not the taxpayer agrees with his findings.

If there is a discrepancy resulting from the findings, the regional officer will make the proper assessment based on best evidence obtainable, to come up with a computation of the deficiency tax. Hence, a PAN (Preliminary Assessment Notice) will be served.

ASSESSMENT INVOLVING FACTUAL ISSUES

There are factual issues that are subject of assessment:
- If expense is not supported by receipts or invoices
- Deducted expense is personal to taxpayer
- If there was under-withholding of taxes, or if there are expenses subject to withholding taxes but were not withheld
- Unallowable expense account deducted from gross income
- A tax credit certificate that was not attached to the tax return
- When income tax return does not tally with VAT and withholding tax returns
- Undeclared income or unallowable deduction was claimed

Period of Limitation or Prescription for Assessment and Collection

Sec. 203 – Except as provided in Section 222, internal revenue taxes shall be assessed within three (3) years after the day prescribed by law for the filling of the return, and no proceeding in court without assessment for the collection of such taxes shall begin after the expiration of such period: Provided, that in a case where a return is filed beyond the period prescribed by law, the three (3) year period shall be counted from the day the return was filed. For purposes of this section, a return filed before the day prescribed by law for the filing thereof shall be considered as filed on such day.

Note: Sec. 203 of the NIRC provides for the prescription period where the government specially the BIR can assess or collect taxes from the taxpayer. Basically, the prescription period for assessment shall be 3 years and the prescription for the collection of taxes shall also be 3 years from the time of the assessment or from the time the return is filed. If the return is filed before the last day of filing, it shall be considered as filed on the last day for purposes of the prescription. Therefore, the right of the government to collect taxes can prescribe by the omission or neglect of BIR officials.

Sec. 222 sets an exception to the prescription of assessment and collection on some grounds as stated in paragraph [a]. Such grounds are;

1. falsity in the return
2. fraudulent return with intent to evade tax
3. failure to file a return

The prescription period for assessment on any of the grounds stated shall be ten [10] years from discovery. The prescription for collection of such assessed tax shall be five [5] years from the time of assessment.

Revenue regulation 12-99 was promulgated to implement the provision on the assessment of taxes and to provide the rules governing the extrajudicial settlement of a taxpayer's criminal violation of the said code or its implementing regulations through the payment of a suggested compromise penalty.

The Due Process Requirement in the Issuance of a Tax Assessment

Mode of procedures in the issuance of a deficiency tax assessment

1. Notice for Informal Conference

– The Revenue Officer who audited the taxpayer's records shall 'among others' state in his report whether or not the taxpayer agrees with his findings. Based on the said Officer's submitted report, the taxpayer shall be informed, in writing, by the Revenue District Office or by the special Investigation Division, as the case may be (by Revenue Regional Offices or by the chief of Division concerned) of the discrepancy or discrepancies in the taxpayer's payment of his internal revenue taxes. The object is to afford the tax payer with an opportunity to respond to the case. If the taxpayer fails to respond within fifteen (15) days from date of receipt of receipt of the notice for informal, he shall be considered in default, in which case, the Revenue District Office or the chief of the special Investigation Division of the Revenue Regional Office or the Chief of Division in the Office, as the case may be, shall endorse the case with the least possible delay to the Assessment Division of the Revenue Office or the commissioner or his duly authorized representative, as the case may be, for appropriate review and Issuance of a Tax Assessment if warranted.

2. Preliminary Assessment Notice

If after review and evaluation by the Assessment Division or by the Commissioner or his duly authorized representative, as the case may be, it is determined that tax is unpaid, the said office shall issue to the taxpayer, at least by registered mail a Preliminary Assessment Notice (PAN) for the proposed assessment, showing in detail, the facts and law, rules and regulations, or jurisprudence on which the proposed assessment is based. If the taxpayer fails to respond within fifteen (15) days from receipt of the PAN, he shall be considered in default, in which case, a formal letter of demand and assessment notice shall be caused to be issued by the Office, calling for payment of the taxpayer's deficiency tax liability, inclusive of the application penalties.

3. **Formal Letter of Demand and Assessment Notice –**

The formal letter of demand and assessment notice shall be issued by the commissioner or his duly authorized representative. The letter of demand calling for payment of the taxpayer's deficiency tax or taxes shall state the facts, the law, rules and regulations, or jurisprudence on which the assessment is based; otherwise, the formal letter of demand and assessment notice shall be void. The same shall be sent to the taxpayer only by registered mail or by personal delivery. If sent by personal delivery, the taxpayer or his duly authorized representative shall acknowledge receipt thereof in duplicate copy of the letter of demand, showing the following: 1) his name; 2) signature; 3) designation and authority to act on behalf of the taxpayer, if acknowledgment is received by a person other than the taxpayer himself; 4) date of receipt thereof.

4. Disputed Assessment

How to Dispute the Formal Letter of Demand and Assessment Notice: - the taxpayer or his duly authorized representation may protest administratively against the aforesaid formal letter of demand and assessment notice within thirty [30] days from date of receipt thereof. If there are several issues involved in the formal letter of demand and assessment notice but the taxpayer only disputes or protests against the validity of some of the issues raised, the taxpayer shall be required to pay the deficiency tax or taxes attributable to the undisputed issues, in which case, a collection letter shall be issued to the taxpayer calling for payment of the said deficiency tax, inclusive of the applicable surcharge and\or interest. No action shall be taken on the taxpayer's undisputed issue.

    a. The prescriptive period for assessment and collection of tax attributable to the disputed issues shall be suspended. The taxpayer shall submit the required documents in support of his protest within sixty [60] days from date of filing of his letter of protest, otherwise, the assessment shall become final, executory and demandable. If the taxpayer fails to file a valid protest on the formal letter of demand and assessment notice within thirty [30] days from date of receipt thereof, the assessment shall become final, executory and demandable.

b. If the protest is denied, on the whole or in part, by the commissioner, taxpayer may appeal to the Court of Tax Appeals within thirty [30] days from date of receipt of the said decision, otherwise, the assessment shall become final, executory and demandable. If the Commissioner or his duly authorized representative fails to act on the taxpayers protest 180 days from date of submission of the required documents in support of his protest, the taxpayer may appeal to the Court of Tax Appeal within thirty [30] days from the lapse of the said 180 days period, otherwise, the assessment shall become final executory and demandable.

"No Tax on Work" and Other Reflections on Public Finance

Veredigno Atienza

Introduction

First of all, let me thank all of you for finding the time to be with us this morning. This is the second Monthly Business Forum of Barangay San Lorenzo Business Association,

Our topic today is "No Tax on Work and Other Reflections on Public Finance". As president of BSLBA and as president of the Philippine Taxpayers Union, I will be your speaker for this forum.

Let us welcome our guests from China led by Mr. Fengjiang Liu. Their organization is the Beijing International Tax Research Society, with a total membership of 120,000, consisting of taxpayers, tax administrators, and tax consultants. Their organization and the Philippine Taxpayers Union are both members of the World Taxpayers Associations and co-founding members of the Asia-Pacific Taxpayers Union. We in the PTU with a membership of less than 100 and in the BSLBA with a membership of less than 6,000 are humbled by the size of our guest association. Nonetheless, we hope that they will find their stay with us fruitful and pleasant.

It is with great appreciation and humility that we welcome our friends from China as we also welcome officials of Barangay San Lorenzo especially

Chairman Jay Santiago, my fellow directors and members from BSLBA, especially our BSLBA members who are attending our Monthly Forum only for the first time.

In our 2006 email correspondence, I had informed Mr. Fengjiang Liu of our tax-related topic in the BSLBA Monthly Forum. He saw this as a wonderful opportunity to learn from us and perhaps also for us to learn from them. We are allowing enough time for an open forum after my presentation. We hope that our BSLBA and PTU members and other guests will also find valuable insights in our forum today. Without further ado, let me proceed.

Two Years Ago

At this point, let me go back two years in time. Two years ago, in January 2005, the Philippines was gripped in a fiscal crisis. The government was then looking at the increase of the value-added tax rate from 10% to 12%, as the key move necessary to cure the budget deficit and the fiscal crisis.

Around the same time, in January 2005, Bjorn Tarras-Wahlberg, founder and presently secretary-general of the World Taxpayers Associations, and formerly president of the Swedish Taxpayers Association, paid a visit for the first time to the Philippines. In November 2004, the Philippine Taxpayers Union had been accepted as the Philippine member of the World Taxpayers Associations. We in the PTU were fortunate that Mr Wahlberg decided to add a Philippine segment to his planned visit to Beijing and Shanghai in 2005.

We considered Mr Wahlberg's visit a great opportunity for WTA and the PTU to contribute to the then raging debate on VAT or the EVAT at the time. We lined up speaking engagements, press conferences, and TV interviews for Mr. Wahlberg. His opinions were covered in the columns of Alvin Capino and Dan Mariano, and in several early-morning radio programs. Mr. Wahlberg and I were separately interviewed in two consecutive programs by ABS-CBN's ANC Channel. It is self-serving for us in WTA and PTU to claim that Mr. Wahlberg and PTU made a significant difference, but his visit helped one way or the other.

In his talks, Mr Wahlberg was in favor of the expanded value-added tax plan of the government. Compared to the VAT rates of other countries, he found our 12% rate still low and reasonable. As a consumption tax, he believed that the VAT was easier to collect and administer compared to the income tax. He also believed that the VAT or EVAT was pro-poor for as long as the EVAT will not apply to fresh produce, books, and other products bought at large by the poor.

The Philippine experience of 2005 and 2006 proved the wisdom of the expanded value-added tax, very much in line with the opinions and observations of Mr Wahlberg. Presently, the Philippine peso is at 48.66 pesos to a US dollar, the strongest in six-years. The basic economic indicators show greater strength compared to previous years, such as the inflation rate, interest rates, and the budget deficit. Property prospects have not been as positive and encouraging as now since 1997.

Mr. Wahlberg also emphasized that there should be less brackets for our income tax, and he introduced the recent experiences of other countries, particularly the Eastern European countries that have converted to capitalism, including Russia. These countries have adopted the flat tax, otherwise known as bracketless tax, which has only one rate as the basis of extracting the tax payable out of the income earned by the taxpayer.

In the Philippines, we do not have any experience yet with less income tax brackets or with flat and bracketless income tax. However, the favorable experiences of other countries, and the increased adoption of flatter tax rates, if not outright flat tax by other countries, is a powerful argument for a more serious look at these tax concepts.

No Tax on Work

Even as Mr. Wahlberg was proposing a higher VAT, and greater emphasis on VAT compared to income taxes, plus lower income taxes and flatter tax rates, PTU suggested to him that ultimately the ideal tax system is not to have any tax on income altogether, whether the income is personal or corporate. Mr. Wahlberg found our idea of "no tax on work" very radical, but very promising.

To be candid and humble about it, the idea of "no tax on work" is not exactly original. Offshore tax havens have discovered the idea a long time ago. Furthermore, some states in the United States do not have any income tax such as Nevada. Even furthermore, there are various bills pending in the United States Congress, which propose the elimination of the income tax and the conversion to a national sales tax.

Common sense seems to dictate that it is more practical to tax consumption, rather than income. From our own Philippine experience, even the man in the street will tell us that consumption is always more conspicuous than income generation. We do not really know how people earn their income and build up their wealth, but it is easy to see if someone is making a lot of money, simply by the way he spends.

There are other considerations, perhaps philosophical, and therefore more strategic. Though taxes are the lifeblood of the government, work is the lifeblood of the nation. A government can collect only so much from the people. Unless work is promoted and increased, there will be a serious limit to the amount of taxes that can be collected. Since work is more basic than taxation, the encouragement of work should take precedence over taxation. One way of doing this is to minimize if not altogether abolish all tax on work and on anything that promotes the creation of work.

In specific terms, we refer to the abolition of all income taxes, both personal and corporate, and the minimization of any and all taxes on business.

Since it is hard to collect taxes from variable-income earners, such as doctors, lawyers, accountants, dealmakers, advisors, salespeople, movie stars, other entertainers, et al, let us altogether forget trying to collect from them. In the spirit of fairness, let us also cease to collect taxes from our fixed-income personnel such as employees, clerks, workers, managers and executives. Similarly those working in the government such as soldiers, police, teachers, clerks, supervisors, bureau directors, even Cabinet secretaries and elected officials should be spared from paying income taxes, as we spare those in the private sector.

Likewise, since corporations have the resources including tax lawyers, tax accountants, tax advisors, et al, that allow them to circumvent income taxation, while costing the government substantial expenses to try to collect such taxes on income, it will be more economical and will yield a higher return to government efforts if income taxes are abolished and replaced.

Since work is dependent on capital for its creation, it is also logical that all taxes on deposits, savings, investments, insurance and pre-need plans should also be abolished. Social security deductions and contributions are not included since they are not taxes on work, but serve as investments for the emergency and long-term benefits of employees.

Following the "no tax on work" concept, it thereby makes sense to review the whole range of business taxes, the marginal rates of business taxation, the number of exemptions and allowances, the corresponding business tax compliance and administration costs, the complexity of tax legislation in general, the complexity of tax administration in general, the ratio of total business taxes to gross profits, the days needed to pay taxes, the number of steps needed to pay taxes, the number of private-public interactions required to settle and pay taxes, the number of forms and pages needed to pay taxes.

Not Exactly Dreaming

Though we are not tax accountants, tax lawyers, tax consultants, tax economists, tax administrators, or any other type of tax professional, being taxpayers we have the right to voice our opinions and to present options. Being livelihood earners, we know something about how taxation and public finance affect our livelihoods and pocketbooks. Practical experience helps us ordinary people to generate new notions about taxation. Definitely, nothing is cast in stone in taxation and in public finance. Besides, we are not exactly dreaming when we talk of what we talk about.

On the ground, we ordinary taxpayers and businessmen have seen that there seems to be a dual economy. There is a segment of the economy that profits much from boom periods and is barely affected when boom turns to bust. And there is another segment, perhaps divisible into further sub-segments, which barely benefits during the boom periods, and suffers greatly during the bust period. There is a great disconnect somewhere.

In the year 2006, the growth rate of Philippine GNP was estimated at 5.5%. In contrast, the Social Weather Station showed a higher rate of Filipinos claiming poverty and hunger. Whether we look in the countryside or in the inner cities, many Filipinos are not in the loop. They are not just marginalized, they are excluded, they are simply not included.

To say that "some people are simply smarter or faster" leads us nowhere. Education is also important, but may take one or more generations to solve the social problems. The answer it seems to us is to directly confront the problem of lack of livelihood.

To have more livelihoods, there simply has to be more jobs and more businesses. How? Thru the elimination of personal and corporate income taxes and business taxes in the long-term, and the movement of personal and corporate income taxation to a flatter, if not bracketless arrangement, in the short and medium term.

Less personal and corporate taxes will expand the domestic market, and will give salary and wage earners greater income that can be directed to savings and to direct and indirect investments. Similarly, what applies to individuals can apply to companies, which will experience an expansion of their domestic markets, and generate greater profits and more savings that can be used for re-investment. For the government, a simpler income tax system will mean more savings and more collections. A flat tax system will mean further and even more savings and collections for the government. As for those companies that have remained outside Philippine shores, they will re-compute their own Philippine profit potential, due to the expansion of the domestic market and the greater retention of profits for re-investment.

Solving the Disconnect

If the tax system of the Philippines can be made less dependent on income taxation in particular and on business taxation in general, and if government expenditures can be focused on meaningful infrastructure (roads, bridges, dams, ports, airports, rails, telecoms, courtrooms) and investment in human capital such as education, health, and shelter (schools, hospitals, training centers, socialized housing), with minimized graft and corruption and a resized bureaucracy, then the Philippines will have the most relevant, the most progressive, and most productive system of public finance in its history.

This kind of public finance will solve the problem of disconnect between the more agile, more prosperous, and more included segments of Philippine society and the less prosperous, more marginalized and less able segments of our economy and society.

Public finance is the answer to the problems of the Philippines. To make public finance work, taxpayer groups and taxpayer associations have to be organized at all levels of our society, and in every nook and cranny of our archipelago. Homeowner associations, parishes, corporations, professional associations, socio-civic groups, credit unions, and any meaningful form of human assembly should have a taxpayer group or tax association.

Taxpayer Associations

One hallmark of progressive countries is the level of development and maturity of their taxpayer associations, taxpayer groups or taxpayer unions. More developed countries believe that public finance is too important to leave in the hands of the government. The sociology of taxation and public finance is a critical aspect in ensuring that taxation and government expenditures are for the interest of the people not of a few vested interests.

Replacement for Income Taxation

There are realistic replacements for income taxation, and this is consumption taxation (value-added taxes, sales tax, customs duties, and excise taxes). With regard to consumption taxation, sales taxes are less cumbersome than value-added taxation.

In the shorter run, for a better way to meet its tax revenue targets, the government should seek to lower its tax rates and to simplify the tax schemes. In 2001, Russia a former communist country lowered its corporate income tax rate from 35% to 24%, and lowered and simplified taxation for small business. Tax revenues increased by 15% per annum from 2001 to 2005.

Eastern European and Central Asian countries that have gotten out of the Soviet Union have reduced their income tax rates and have seen their tax revenues rise: Bulgaria, Kazakhstan, Slovakia, Moldova, Latvia, Romania. (Note: Bulgaria and Romania have just joined the European Union.) In 2004, Georgia reduced tax rates and simplified its tax system. In 2005, only 11% of businesses surveyed in Georgia reported the need for bribery, compared to 44% in 2002.

Key tax reforms are sweeping different countries. The most dramatic actual reform has been the introduction of the flat tax. The pioneer was Estonia in 1994 with a flat tax of 26%, with Slovakia following in 2003, Romania and Georgia in 2004.

Aside from lower rates, an electronic manner of filing must be encouraged, as in Singapore, where filing taxes is practically paperless and is reputed to require only a day to complete. In Switzerland, it takes one page per quarter and one day a year to handle the filing of VAT returns.

Ultimately, in the long run taxation all over the world will have to be a combination of value-added taxation and sales taxation, administered as simply as possible. A 1% tax on gross sales is practically a 20% tax on net income before tax (NIBT) where NIBT is 5% of gross sales, but is easier to compute and administer compared to income taxation, and can apply to practically all types of businesses. Value-added taxation can provide for differences in various types of business. If income tax were still to be included, a flat tax or bracketless tax would be an efficient complement to sales taxation and value-added taxation. As for the flat income tax, it should be brought down lower and lower, until it is gone.

For as long as the basic products bought by the poor are exempted from consumption tax – eg fresh produce, sugar, salt, books, medical services, and for as long as the requirements for compliance do not evolve to be more and more cumbersome, VAT and the whole range of consumption taxation should be the basis for the generation of government revenue for the Philippines and other countries as well. As governments try to compete with one another in bringing down the cost of doing business in their home turf, and as the competition for international investments continues, VAT and consumption taxes can be expected to dominate.

In conclusion, we can say that "no tax on work" is not just a philosophy, but also a strategy and a necessity in a world that is getting to be smaller and smaller, and more competitive. "No tax on work" is not just wishful thinking. It can be done. "No tax on work" is not just an idea of ordinary people who know little about tax rulings, regulations and procedures, but an idea whose time has come, an idea that should permeate and dominate public policy.

Taxation is definitely not the most exciting topic in the world especially on a nice Friday morning like this when the week end is almost here. Rest assured however that taxation and public finance are very important to your lives and fortunes. Please please please be more involved in these areas. Please organize taxpayer groups in your respective spheres of influence. Follow the public money since it is your money. Thank you for your attention.

Veredigno Atienza
BSLBA Monthly Business Forum
January 12, 2007

Abolishing Income Taxes, Retaining Consumption Taxes

Why income taxes can be abolished,
Consumption taxes as main government
revenue source[1]

Bienvenido "Nonoy" Oplas, Jr.[2]

A. Philosophy/Principle

1. Economic activities by productive individuals and enterprises always (a) create jobs, and (b) expand production of food, housing, clothing, transportation, other human needs. Hence, they already serve welfare functions to society, and they should not be penalized with income taxes and bureaucratic licenses and permits.

2. There are plenty of consumption-based taxes already in place. In particular: (a) value added tax or VAT, (b) sales tax, (c) excise tax, (d) import tax, (e) vehicle registration tax, (f) real property tax, (g) percentage tax, (h) amusement tax, (i) travel tax, among others.

3. In addition, various bureaucracy-generated taxes, like (a) documentary stamp tax, (b) franchise tax, (c) bank earnings witholding tax, (d) insurance premium tax, (e) business permit tax, (f) fire code tax, and so on.

4. Very bureaucratic, discretionary, costly and corruption-prone to fully enforce income tax collections since people do not want to divulge their true income; cheaper to hire good accountants and

lawyers and bribe revenue collectors than pay the full income tax liability. What the current income tax laws only affect are the fixed-income earners like teachers, office employees, soldiers, and so on.

5. Welfare loss to society = income taxes paid + cost of compliance (hiring accountants, lawyers, other business consultants) + cost of bribery (to avoid paying taxes or bring down their tax liabilities).

6. In addition, many people who live off on taxes, like those working in multilateral institutions (UN, WB, IMF, ADB), in other governments' foreign aid bodies and embassies, are exempted from mandatory withholding income taxes. The more reason that those working in the private sector, those who derive their income not from taxes of other people but on business sales, should be spared from paying income tax.

B. The Numbers

1. Collections from income tax (P Billion, except %)

(a) From Individuals
2005, 112.68
2006, 132.01
2007, 154.30

(b) From corporations, enterprises, others
2005, 210.75
2006, 263.22
2007, 300.07

Percent of (a) to total tax revenues
2005, 16.0%
2006, 15.0%

2007, 12.8%

Percent of (a+b) to total tax revenues
2005, 45.8%
2006, 44.8%
2007, 37.6%

Total tax revenues *
2005, 705.61
2006, 881.62
2007, 1,208.20

* Not included here are (i) "non-tax revenues" like various fees and charges, Bureau of Treasury (BTr) income, privatization proceeds, and (ii) local government taxes and fees.

(Source: Budget of Expenditures and Sources of Financing (BESF), 2007)

2. GDP computation

Gross Domestic Product (GDP) is the sum of household consumption (C), government consumption (G), private and government investment (I) and net exports (X-M). Alternatively, GDP is also computed as the sum of gross value added (GVA) of agriculture, industry and services sectors. Or:

GDP = C + I + G + (X-M), or
GDP = GVA Agri + GVA Industry + GVA Services.

Nominal GDP figures were:
2003, P4,316 B; 2004, P4,859 B; 2005, P5,419 B; 2006, P6,025 B.

3. Assumptions when income taxes, at least personal income tax, is zero:

(a) informal or underground economy will fall from 43% ** (WB estimates) to around 20% of GDP (or 80% formal economy); and

(b) GDP growth will be higher as household consumption (C) will increase. And C comprises nearly 75% of GDP; and

(c) VAT to be augmented by a national sales tax, composite consumption tax of 12%; and

(d) all other consumption-based taxes are retained; exemptions to VAT retained.

(** Note: Main culprit for the high incidence of informal sector is the high and multiple taxes and fees, the many permits and licenses to secure with various government agencies, both national and local government units)

4. Projected revenue collections under zero income tax, expanded consumption taxes, on a P8 trillion GDP:

(a) Taxable national income = (nominal GDP) x (formal economy)= (P8 trillion) x (0.80) = P6.4 trillion

(b) Projected collections from VAT & sales tax alone = (taxable income) x (12% VAT & sales tax)= (P6.4 trillion) x (0.12) = P768 billion.
This is equivalent to projected collections of (i) income tax + (ii) general sales & VAT. Projected revenue from (i + ii) in 2007 is P628 billion. As discussed earlier, there are other tax revenues which will not be affected

by this initiative, like proceeds from excise tax, franchise tax, property tax.

C. Conclusion

1. One major impact of zero income tax, especially on personal income, is large-scale job creation. A household with combined withholding tax of say, P6,000/month will experience an equivalent "wage increase" of the same amount. That amount will be used to hire a "yaya" (nanny) or housemaid, or to increase food consumption if the family size is big, creating new jobs in the food production sectors.

2. In addition, many employees who dream of becoming employers and job creators someday will find it easier to realize their dreams. They do not have to borrow much money as they can save their de facto "pay rise" in the form of zero income tax, for bigger equity in their entrepreneurial project someday.

3. Society's human resources will be reallocated to more productive use. There will be less tax collection bureaucrats, less demand for tax consulting services (accounting, legal, PR, etc.) as the taxation system is more simple. If those bureaucrats and income tax consulting guys are into productive enterprises instead, then society's production of more goods and services will expand, further creating more job opportunities.

4. People often hide their source of income, or how much they're earning. But they flaunt their consumption – big house, big or fast cars, expensive clothes and cellphones, throwing parties, frequent travels and vacation, and so on. Taxing people on their consumption is much easier to administer because they

give clear hints of their consumption preferences.

5. Low-income people who paid no or low income tax and low consumption tax before will not be worse off in a new situation where consumption taxes are higher. With plenty of job opportunities around, moving to high-paying jobs should be easier if one has sufficient ambition and industriousness.

6. Ultimately, consumption tax and other taxes must come down; some will have to be abolished too (as income taxes remain zero) – in a regime of small government, and bigger personal responsibilities and bigger role for voluntary organizations and civil society.

D. Timetable

1. The main goal of this taxpayers' movement is a law that will abolish income tax, and shift revenue collection to consumption-based taxes.

2. To lessen drastic revenue adjustments, that law need not provide outright drop in income tax rate from the current 32% to zero in one year. A phase-in period of gradual reduction from 32% to zero in a period of 5 to 10 years as sales tax increase is being worked out will be instituted.

3. Meanwhile, the immediate task is to expand the number of individuals and organizations who will support this single goal. Existing organizations can affiliate with PTU. Or individuals who do not belong to any organization can form their own local taxpayers association or union (say, Pasig Taxpayers Association) and affiliate with PTU.

4. If we are strong enough, we can push a bill this year, and expect a law within 2 to 3 years (2008 or 2009).

[1] Presented during the forum on "In Search of a National Consensus", sponsored by the Barangay San Lorenzo Business Association (BSLBA), at My Cinema, Greenbelt 3, Makati City, March 30, 2007.

Note: Nonoy Oplas is Secretary-General of the Philippine Taxpayers Union and President of the Minimal Government Movement

Zero Income Tax

Rene Azurin

"Zero income tax" has a nice melodic sound. It produces in me the same resonant vibrations as Toyota's "zero defect" production system and the environmentalist movement's "zero waste" program. So, given the current hoohah over the BIR's latest failure to meet its tax collection targets, it seems timely to propose that hard-to-collect income taxes be now scrapped altogether and the revenue derived therefrom raised instead through easier- to-collect consumption taxes. This replaces a messy, susceptible-to-**corruption** system with a simpler, less discretionary one.

I have actually been suggesting this for many years now to any tax official who would listen so I was very glad to learn that my friend and former graduate school classmate, Dr. Veredigno Atienza, has created an advocacy group to lobby for this to happen. The organization founded by Dr. Atienza is called the Philippine Taxpayers Union and it is affiliated with the World Taxpayers Associations, a movement now in 42 countries that grew "out of the desire of citizens to protect themselves from the increasing tax claims of the state."

I think that is an excellent reason for citizens to band together. Taxes, after all, are forcible impositions made by those with power on those without it. From a historical perspective, these are qualitatively no different from the tong extorted from people by the ancient predatory bandits who called themselves kings.

In fact, taxes can be effectively looked at as the goods that the productive members of the community are compelled to give up in order to support the lifestyles of a non-productive group of individuals sometimes called politicos.

Of course, in a modern democracy, taxes are supposed to be payments for certain support services - like maintaining order and administering the system of justice - performed by the politicos who capture control of government power. Accordingly, citizens are well in their rights to demand that the goods they are forced to give up are used in the proper manner and not used to enrich parasitic politicos who think that they are entitled to lavish compensation for what they imagine is productive work.

From a practical standpoint, however, citizens have no real power to make that demand - since politicos wield the coercive instruments and armed might of the state - and this is why it is necessary for individual citizens to band together to achieve a modicum of power possible through concerted group action.

The WTA and its member associations like the PTU support initiatives that "limit tax burdens, prevent unjust harassment by tax collectors, and provide clear information about government taxation and expenditure."

In a recent forum organized by Dr. Atienza, PTU Secretary-General Bienvenido Oplas, Jr. presented a paper arguing for the abolition of income taxes and making consumption taxes the main source of government revenue. Principally, he argued that income tax collection is "very bureaucratic, discretionary, costly, and **corruption**-prone...[because] people do not want to divulge their true income...[and it is] cheaper to hire good accountants and lawyers and **bribe** revenue collectors than pay the full income tax liability." Additionally, Oplas argued that individuals and enterprises that engage in economic activities - by producing goods, services, and jobs - "already serve welfare functions in society...and they should not be penalized with income taxes and bureaucratic licenses and permits."

I agree completely. Taxes based on consumption are simpler to administer since these are collected from merchants and businesses which constitute a far smaller number than the number of individual taxpayers. Consumption taxes are also inherently fairer. The more you consume, the more taxes you pay. Moreover, this is more consistent with individual freedom because it allows each consumer to spend all that he earns in a manner that maximizes his satisfaction while still generating for the government the required amounts to fund support services. To address social welfare concerns, consumption tax rates can be set higher for non- essentials like cars and condos, and lower for essentials like food and medicine. Certain basic commodities like rice and galunggong can even be exempt from any consumption taxes whatsoever.

If one grants that the present national budget of some P1.1 trillion is a reasonable imposition on the producing classes of our society, then the required tax bite will amount to some 17% of the aggregate value of goods and services produced domestically (assuming a GDP of around P7 trillion). The amount in tax take to be foregone from the abolition of personal and corporate income taxes - I believe this was around P881 billion in 2006 - can actually be drawn from various consumption-based taxes already being collected like value-added taxes, sales taxes, excise taxes, real property taxes, vehicle registration taxes, travel taxes, amusement taxes, and import duties. How this is to be distributed just takes a little arithmetic.

One might also argue, however, as PTU does, that scrapping income taxes will actually expand the total tax base and therefore allow a desired tax take to be raised with not too high an increase in the prevailing rates of existing consumption-based taxes. The argument made is that zero income taxes will stimulate business investment, generate greater economic activity, and bring currently underground businesses (the so-called informal economy) out into the open. This can mean increased government revenues even with lower taxes per taxpayer. And there will be less **corruption**. In the end, this translates into faster growth for the economy as a whole.

So, citizens, let us band together and support this initiative. A zero income tax system is good for all of us. But not, maybe, for some people in government.

SECTION NINE: REFLECTIONS

Icons Then and Now

Kuku Lopez

A few days ago, I was walking in the school corridor to meet up with my mentor in research methods when I heard somebody say: "He's so iconic!" Iconic? Come to think of it, I see the word a lot nowadays in the lifestyle section of many newspapers and magazines. It brings me to mull over what is in a word.

Well, big words terrify me. Tiny words unfamiliar to the memory and the tongue intimidate me. But somehow, after half a century, I learned to live with both of them. I roll them in my tongue. I chew them with gusto. And many times, I eat them, of course, I spit them out too. Big and tiny words, oh, I trip over them like nobody's business. I not only forget when to cross my T's, but I also run roughshod over my grammar. I watch myself very carefully because I would not want to greet a friend saying: "Hi where did you went?"

Words like icon would have made me scurry to the corner, but thanks to the nuns who hovered over me in my childhood, I got the word right in the spelling bee contest when I was in Grade III. I also knew its meaning! Icons were those golden curlicued crosses and blonde, kinky-haired images at the school chapel which the manangs would polish. I always wondered though why they hushed me every time I went near anyone of those.

My mother had one too – a foot-high antique ivory image of Mary, very life-like in features with eyes made of glass. Her tiny hands looked so delicate with tiny, tiny fingers so lovingly sculpted.

Icons could be very tiny too. We had this very small headless image, probably of a saint, that glowed in the dark. The closet was our favorite hangout, where we waited for this glowing icon to levitate off our hands. Well, we kept on going back to the closet and we waited for a long, long time but the icon stayed on our palms, glowing but immobile. So we decided, heck, it's time to grow up.

Webster says 'icon' started as a Greek word for image. For many years, icons were associated with religious images and were looked upon by many as stand-ins for the real ones in heaven. You wipe their feet with perfumed handkerchiefs and kiss them softly. The kids usually take a fast peck at their feet and squirm out of their mothers' hold more interested in climbing the "campanarios." (You should try it – the view is glorious up there. Of course, I got some tongue-lashing from the nuns for almost killing them with fright!) You walk on your knees from the church door to the altar with your eyes focused on their lovely faces.

In these modern times, I would like to venture that the word icon still represents something – pictorially or visually – but instead of being confined to just religious images, the word now could refer to any representation of a specific aspect of the social system.

The collapse of many traditions and conventions brought about by the numerous revolutions – industrial, religious, scientific, political, social, cultural, economic, (EDSA?) – created what can perhaps be best described as a fuzzy, gray area where icons could be anything or anyone. Whichever representation it may be, these present-day icons still evoke just as much emotion and passion and dedication from their cultish following who wish to take them into their hearts and minds.

So you have Magsaysay, Quezon, Ninoy, Salonga, Evelio, FVR, Atang, Carmen, Rogelio, Gloria, Luis (or Juancho), Susan, Fernando, Amalia, Romeo, Erap et al, Ai-ai, Mike Enriquez, Susan Enriquez (no relation to Mike), Mel and Jay, Paolo, Vicky, Bernadette, Karen Davilla, Arnold, Voltes V, Tamaguchi, Angel Locsin, Kristine Hermosa, Tessa Prieto Valdes, Maurice, Tito, Vic, Joey, Nene Tamayo, sino at ano pa? – endless enumeration of heroic angels and fallen angels, animate and inanimate, local and foreign, hennaed and otherwise – all of them leading the pack.

One gets to wonder if the animates ever stopped to think how they have so captured the hearts and minds of so many. Do they realize the power they hold in their hands? Icons have vast powers. Because their followers look up to them– as representations of the dreams and aspirations of them who are still clawing their way out of their miserable holes, icons have the power to change somebody's life by being mindful of how they conduct themselves. Or icons can destroy a life by being mindless in their deeds. Icons can so easily bring a whole nation to smithereens. And when one thinks that many of them can be so mindless, I regress and wish for that headless icon that glowed in the dark and, maybe, just maybe – if I pray hard enough and wait long enough – I will be the one to levitate.

Chacha & Other Dances

Veredigno Atienza

If I had my druthers, I would prefer a presidential-parliamentary system with a federalist touch. Of course, we ordinary folks can just shoot the breeze. We can give our opinions, but I wonder how much of these will matter, even if these come out in a newspaper called Linkages, with an assured circulation of 10,000 readers.

At any rate, we can imagine, and we can make suggestions. As to who cares, it does not really matter. We are just exercising a constitutional right, namely our freedom of expression, as well as contributing to the marketplace of ideas.

In some of my yahoo groups, around the same time that the ConCom was being convened, I had sent out a write-up, describing my ideal form of government, my dream government structure. Without referring to anybody in particular, in other words without getting personal, I would rather that the presidential system be retained as the backbone of the new form of government. More specifically, I refer to the retention of the executive department as it is presently structured. As a corollary, the judicial system stays as it is set up. The biggest possibility for change seems to lie in the legislative branch.

Thinking about the unthinkable, wouldn't it be a nice idea if we abolished both houses of congress? From the fiscal point of view, that would mean a lot of savings.

But who or what would replace Congress? How about having a Council of Governors and citizen-legislators?

How is a Council of Governors supposed to function and what animal is this? And what are citizen-legislators?

Simply put, our legislature can be replaced by a Council of Governors, consisting of all the provincial governors, with each governor carrying a vote of one for every 500,000 people in his province. Thus, a governor with a population of 5,000,000 will carry ten votes in the Council of Governors.

The Council of Governors can be scheduled to meet four times a year, for two weeks every quarter, or two times a year, for duration of one month per semester. During their sessions, they discuss and vote. Most of the spade work is done via cyberspace during the other weeks, with votation as the key activity during the weeks in session.

Our citizens can be deputized as legislators, with powers to propose bills thru ICT-based templates. As for getting the bills into law, the Governors will champion the bills they find relevant. Who runs the province when the Council of Governors is in session in Manila? I suppose the provincial administrator or the Vice-Governor.

Who works on the bills in between sessions? The proponent citizen-legislator and the staff of the governor-champion, likely with the help of the provincial boards, the city boards, the municipal boards, and the barangay councils. Between sessions, they propose, lobby, explain, present, and get commitments for the bills they hope to get turned into law during the session. Considering the number of Filipinos who write letters to the editors, who join yahoo groups, who love to banter on ways to save the country, this country will never run out of volunteer citizen-legislators.

Now the tough question: who gets to be the head of state and government? Will the two positions be lodged with one person? Will there be a role for a prime minister?

In our dream system, the president is the head of state, with two primary powers: chair of the commission on elections and commander-in-chief of the armed forces; the rest of his or her functions will be ceremonial. The president and vice-president will be elected for a single term, every six years and directly by the people. The vice-president will serve as the president's chief of staff and successor in case of death or severe disability. As Comelec chief, the president is responsible for all elections except the presidential election.

As for the head of government, he or she is the prime minister. The prime minister will be elected by his peers in the Council of Governors. Half of his appointees from the Council of Governors and half from the public at large will comprise his Cabinet.

The governors will be elected every six years; as the Council of Governors, they will be allowed to have three changes of government. If a fourth change is needed before the six-year term of governors is completed, the president can call for gubernatorial elections.

Will this work? I think so, if the system becomes reality. Will it find its way to reality? I doubt it.

Padugo

Veredigno Atienza

IN THE TOWN OF SAN RAFAEL in the northern part of the province of Bulakan, there is a marker in front of the San Rafael Church. The marker refers to one of the town's three prized treasures, which are: history, tradition and faith in God. This particular marker refers to the town's wealth found in its history.

The marker states that on November 30, 1896, one of the bloodiest battles in the history of Bulakan took place in San Rafael, exactly where the church stood. The battle happened during the Philippine Revolution against Spain. The Filipino Katipuneros were led by a young general named Anacleto Enriquez with the nom de guerre "Matang Lawin" (Hawk-eyed). The Spanish forces were under Lt. Col. Lopez Artiaga.

At the end of the battle, eight hundred Filipino revolutionaries including their leader General Enriquez, lay dead down to the last man with none ever surrendering to the superior force of the Spanish colonial government. The volume of blood spilled in the church reached the ankle ("hanggang bukong-bukong").

Anacleto Enriquez is one of the leading twelve provincial heroes of Bulacan, as mentioned in a resolution of the provincial government. He is not known outside Bulakan.

He was born September 24, 1876 in the town of Bulakan, Bulakan, one of the oldest towns in the

Philippines. His parents were Don Vicente Enriquez y de Jesus and Dona Petrona Sepulvida-Fernando y Gatmaitan. He and his brothers studied at the Ateneo Municipal de Manila. His best friend was fellow Atenean, neighbor, and gangmate Gregorio del Pilar. Like most Ateneans of his time, Anacleto idolized Dr. Jose Rizal, whom Anacleto had a chance to meet at Hotel del Oriente in Manila.

In the month of July 1896, Anacleto and his younger brother Vicente joined the Katipunan. Under orders from Katipunan Supremo Andres Bonifacio, Anacleto went to his hometown of Bulakan to organize the "Balangay Uliran", together with co-founder Doroteo Karagdag. "Balangay Uliran" would merge with "Balangay Apuy" of Malolos to form the "Sangguniang Apuy".

On August 27, 1896, the "Sangguniang Apuy" received orders from Supremo Bonifacio to rise up in arms. In the last years of their Bachillerato courses at the Ateneo, Anacleto and his brother Vicente abandoned their studies to fight for the freedom of their country.

On October 20, 1896, General Isidoro Torres, the head of the Revolutionary Forces in Bulakan, summoned Anacleto to Masukol, Paombong, Bulacan and appointed him second-in-command with the rank of General at the age of 20 years old. His brother Vicente headed the "Uliran" unit, with the rank of Colonel.

Anacleto and Vicente found out the consequences of their decision to fight Spain. The Spanish authorities marked Anacleto as Bulakan's most dangerous military leader. Their sister Victoria was thrown into jail, their mother Petrona was jailed in Bilibid Manila.

The Philippine revolutionaries were ill-prepared for any type of war. They lacked arms, soldiers, training, technology, ammunition, information, experience and strategic savvy. On November 29, 1896, upon the orders of Gen. Torres, Anacleto moved his troops to Hacienda Buenavista (San Ildefonso). Finding Buenavista hard to defend, Anacleto decided to move to San Rafael in the early hours of November 30, 1896.

By seven in the morning, Anacleto's forces were under the strongest artillery and infantry attack unleashed by the Spanish forces since the start of the revolutionary war. Either because all means of escape had been cut off or because they simply preferred death instead of surrender, Anacleto and his men proceeded to the San Rafael Church for their last stand. At noontime, one of the largest military contingents ever mobilized by the Spanish authorities during the Philippine Revolution assaulted the church.

The Spanish forces (Infanterio and Guardia Civil) and the Katipuneros under General Enriquez engaged in hand-to-hand combat. When the smoke cleared, there was blood everywhere, in the sacristia, in the altar area, in the choir area. There were headless bodies, disemboweled bodies and bodyless heads. Intestines were all over with food in different stages of digestion. Blood was ankle-deep, the blood of the rich mixed with the blood of the poor. The blood of Anacleto mixed with the blood of his men, among who was the Enriquez family cochero.

El Diario de Manila carried the news, with special reference to Anacleto Enriquez and how he was found dead, as he clutched in his hand the braided hair of Clara Siapit, the girl he loved and had promised to marry.

Anacleto Enriquez's padugo (blood offering) was pure, unconditional, unqualified. He gave up everything for his country – his life and his bright future, his talents, his time, his education, his share of the family inheritance, even the love of the woman he wanted to marry and of the family he hoped to have. He simply gave. He did not give to give back. He did not give to get anything in return. Measured against the standard of his generosity and heroism, how do we all rate?

Reflections on Teaching

Ma.Corazon Lopez

It is sad to say, as Professor Elmore said, that for many professors, while they have been primed by their education to conduct research, "their only preparation for teaching is their own, largely unexamined, experience as students."

Discussion teaching is essentially a systematic way of constructing a context, an environment for learning from the knowledge and experience of students, rather than exclusively from the canons of disciplinary knowledge. To teach then is to engage our students in the activity of learning; thus, teaching consists of getting students involved in the active construction of knowledge; they are not just passive recipients of factual information but instead are the main and active processors of information which they eventually integrate into their own knowledge database and system of thinking, feeling, caring and doing.

Learning is contextual in at least three senses: new knowledge is acquired by extending and revising prior knowledge; new ideas acquire meaning when they are presented in a coherent relationship with one another; and knowledge becomes usable when it is acquired in situations that entail applications to concrete problem-solving. Thus, a teacher does not only provide inputs of factual information; he or she must also allow and enable students to scrutinize, analyze, evaluate, synthesize, and integrate such factual information into the students' own universe of sensing through an active process of exchange.

Acquisition and application of knowledge are fundamental social acts. In reality, we learn many things through complex social interactions with others and not through reading of operational manuals. And yet, oftentimes, classroom setting minimally encourages social interaction where "individual cognition is preferred over social interaction, abstract manipulation of symbols over concrete application in practical settings, and generalized learning over applications in specific social contexts." As a consequence of such absence of social interaction in the classroom, "learning in school becomes progressively isolated from the kind of learning that affects people's competencies in real life. "

Using these insights as the foundation of the new pedagogy, teaching, then, is essentially a transformational activity aimed at getting students to take charge of their own learning and to make deeply informed judgments about the world. This view comes closest to the translation of the Latin word "educere" - which means to draw forth the results of learning.

The main value that the students get from the classroom is not the knowledge of the subject itself, (oftentimes, you forget the knowledge part); but rather the predisposition to learn, to discover, to ask, to look, to put together.

Thus, the aim of teaching is not only to transmit information, but also to transform students from passive recipients of other peoples' knowledge into active constructors of their own and others' knowledge.

When my eldest son informed us that he would like to teach in high school after his college graduation, my husband and I told him that "Teaching is not a simple transfer of information. As a teacher, you don't teach the facts of life; you teach a way of life and about life itself. Your views in life ride on the subject matter you teach; the subject matter is just the stimulus which triggers the process of learning. Oftentimes, you yourself become your own subject matter; as you give examples; as you live your own example of life."

Thus, if our definition of teaching is that it is a transformational vocation, what then are the skills needed to be discovered or re-discovered, developed or honed by us? Or is it just the skills that we should focus on? Allow me to go through a few in my list.

1.   CULTURE CHANGE

Unless a certain level of openness and acceptance to change is established in the school, then no true and meaningful change towards being a transformational vocation can happen. While impetus for change should be management-driven, openness to change and wanting to change must be shared by everyone.

2.   COLLECTIVE RESPONSIBILITY

Collective responsibility dictates that we make sure learning also happens not only inside the classroom but anywhere within the university by comporting ourselves along the values and code of conduct we have jointly agreed to uphold.

3.   CURRICULUM

If learning is really to happen inside the classroom, the students must be able to see, understand, and appreciate the relevance of the subject matter they are covering vis-à-vis the reality of their environment.

Such effort to fuse into an interrelated and interconnected view a particular subject matter becomes an individual professor's creative exercise rather than a focused plan.

4.   THE TEACHERS

Without teachers, a curriculum remains to be just a collection of documents designed to develop a student along a certain discipline, enumerating courses to be offered and outlining subjects to be covered.

The teachers are the main instruments that would put life into the curriculum by delivering the subject contents through teaching methodologies that would enable the students to learn.   So, what kind of metaskills should we have to be an effective teacher of the 21st Century?

a. The new pedagogy of teaching demands that a teacher, while remaining to be a specialist along her line of expertise, must be able to talk about other disciplines just as well in order to encourage the free flow of questions and discussions inside the classroom. This requires new as well as continuous learning on the part of the teachers. This requires inter-disciplinary discussions to share information and knowledge among colleagues. This requires formal and informal training which needs to be given funding support and de-loading arrangements. This requires giving up some more of our little time remaining to reading new materials, preparing new teaching programs, coming up with new course outlines, and updating our yellowish note cards.

b. In real life, teaching as a process has no hard and fast rules. While there is a supposed science to teaching, the process is essentially defined by the individual teacher and therefore becomes a highly personalized delivery of learning. It is recommended for a teacher to learn the virtue of humility and the skill to open his or her classroom to positive intrusions from his or her colleagues who may have genuine concern to improve the learning process.

c. To enable students to be active participants in the learning process, teachers must transform themselves from being a master in the master-apprentice relationship fostered by the lecture method to being a partner. In a partner role, the teacher allows the students "to explore the intellectual terrain without maps, blazing trails, struggling past obstacles, dealing with disappointments." In short, the classroom process takes on an unstructured format which requires a different classroom management style.

d. The teachers must also be good and effective integrators and synthesizers of ideas so that they may demonstrate to their students how all their inputs have contributed and supported the learning for the day.

e. Teachers must now employ, at the very least, teaching aids such as projected acetates with colorful visuals and graphic representations to catch the attention of the students. Computer-aided instructional materials are also being employed to address the needs of the new generation. This means that teachers must now be computer-literate - proficient in word processing, spreadsheet development and management and in presentation skills.

f. In the one-month Assumption College critical mass workshop in 1997, Professor Eduardo Morato of the Asian Institute of Management introduced the following non-traditional teaching and learning methodologies: case method, brain-storming., synectetics, serendipity walk, and dream analysis.

g. And lastly, in evaluating the development and progress of the students in their learning, the teachers' focus must be re-oriented from what factual information was learned to how the students listen, react, make notes, analyze, negotiate, prepare to pounce, or perhaps to "tune out". This requires a new skill in student evaluation and grading.

May I share with you what Mr. Geerat Vermeij a blind evolutionary biologist who studies sea shells says about his fourth grade Art teacher Mrs. Colberg, who launched Mr. Vermeij's career by tweaking his initial interest in the field of biology through juvenile art projects. He wrote:

"My fourth grade teacher had not only given my hands an unforgettable aesthetic treat, but she aroused in me a lasting curiosity about things unknown. None of it was in the books; there was no expensive conspiracy to teach science, no contrived lesson plan painstakingly conceived by distant experts. Instead, Mrs. Colberg captured the essence of her task. She created an opportunity, a freedom for someone to observe, an encouragement to wonder, and in the end a permissive environment in which to ask a genuine scientific question... A wonderful teacher set the course of one man's life."

Overhaul: A Call for Change of Philippine Society

Ariel Dashell Aaron Tapang Lopez

Over the years, the Filipino people have witnessed changes in the economy and society, some satisfying and reassuring, others turbulent and nerve-wracking. There was a time, in which other South East Asian countries looked up to the Philippines as an economic success, as a success in democracy and capitalism. But looking at the country today, the positive outlook towards the Philippines may have been premature. The years in which the Philippines was once called a "tiger-cub" in the economic playing field, are now far behind. One may even call the Philippine situation bleak and hopeless. But of course, as constantly proven by history, anything is possible. The only thing constant in this world is change.

A wise man once mentioned that a warrior, backed into a corner, is more dangerous than one on the run. For the warrior, who has no place to run, is unpredictable. A person in a corner will have one thing on his mind. And that thought will make him do extraordinary things. It is the idea of survival, of freedom.

The Philippines is indeed being backed into a corner, if not already in one. Political instability prevents the country from being a cohesive force, driving in the direction of success. The country's lawmakers are more concerned with gaining political ground and points, rather than actually getting something done. There's no denying that these politicians do accomplish some things, an infrastructure project here, an education improvement program there. But unfortunately, the political mistakes that they make overshadow what they achieve. Poor execution of laws and policies, the incessant problem of graft and corruption, and a focus on shifting political alliances rather than on accomplishing goals for society, are just some of the problems that plague the system.

The economic scene fares as well as the political one, which isn't really saying much. Though the country may be experiencing an increasing GDP, and an increase of jobs due to the strong influx of the call centre industries, this is by no means a statement that the economic problems have been solved. Problems of tax collection, restrictive economic policies for both foreign and domestic businesses, the existence of an economic system easily manipulated by politics and corruption, continues to plague the country up till now.

Politics and economics have always walked down the path together. A change in one obviously will affect the other. And as we can see with the Philippine example, an unstable political environment will definitely have negative results on the economy. It has taken some time for foreign investors to again place their bets on the Philippines. One need only mention EDSA II and EDSA III. The Oakwood Mutiny, the constant struggle between the government and the various insurgency groups (MILF, CPP-NPA), and the various political scandals like President Arroyo's "Hello Garci" fiasco, make investors think twice about placing their money under the care of the Philippines. The Filipino people continue to live the hard life. And it seems that there is no end in sight.

Indeed, the Philippines is backed into a corner. And of course as always, it is the people's choice whether it chooses to be subdued and ruined in that corner, or whether it focuses all its energy and faces its demons, so as to get out of the corner and gain freedom. It is clear that for the country to be able to see the light again, for the Philippines to be able to climb out of the hole it has dug itself in, it must undergo changes. It must, like a caterpillar before it turns into a butterfly, wrap itself in a cocoon of reflection, so that it can see its problems and deal with them.

Change is always a difficult task to undertake, especially when one is trying to change deeply-rooted ideas and behavior. The Filipino people will have their work cut out for them. It is as much a change in the individual as it is a change in the system. The necessary tasks are the hardest ones to accomplish. But as a phoenix undergoes death through the flame, only to be reborn as a new being full of life, the Philippines and the Filipino people must undertake the hardest task of change, the painful action of looking at one's self to see the flaws, the cracks, the weaknesses, and yes, to fix them.

Values or System Change: Which Comes First?

William M. Esposo

I was one of the panelists invited to the March 30 Annual Forum of the Barangay San Lorenzo Business Association. Following a roundtable format, the Forum had the following topic "In Search of a National Consensus" held at the My Cinema in Greenbelt 3, Makati City.

The other panelists included University of Asia and the Pacific dean Rolly Dy, Philippine Taxpayers Union sec-gen Nonoy Oplas, World Taxpayers Associations sec-gen Bjorn Wahlberg, Ateneo de Manila School of Government asst dean Dennis Gonzales, and fellow columnists Rene Azurin and Bernie Lopez who both write for the BusinessWorld.

My former Ateneo classmate Vernie Atienza invited me to the event which was later televised in the evening on Harry Tambuatco's Insight Inside show over my former network, RPN-9.

Each panelist provided very useful suggestions for a strategic national consensus that will move our country forward. These suggestions are as follows:

1. Less government and more governance which includes the participation of key sectors of society.
2. Electoral reform.

3. Judicial reform.
4. Tax reform.
5. Zero corruption.
6. Values formation.
7. Ethical standards for promotions.
8. Accountability, transparency and good disclosure mechanisms.

This wish list reveals what's so glaringly wrong with the country. Indeed, if all the eight suggestions were achieved, we will not only eradicate the wide scale poverty that has hounded the country for over five decades but we will likely be in step with regional achievers like Singapore.

Bernie Lopez and I believed that we must first overhaul our values as a people before we can bring about a more stable and equitable society. I was for attaining Filipino appreciation of his real history and our core problem which is the wealth gap.

My thesis is that as a people, we find it very hard to even agree on a solution because we ourselves do not have a clear idea on what the real problem is. And we won't appreciate our real problems until we know our real history, recognize who our real friends and enemies are and learn what exactly stunts our development.

A marketing strategist will first need to trace the history of the brand, how it was born, its evolution, from its rise to peak popularity to its present lackluster state before he can start to prescribe solutions. In the world of medicine, a doctor can only heal a serious disease after evaluating a patient's medical history.

Bernie made a superb outline of the elements and dynamics of the clash of values before a good and strategic national consensus can be reached. He delivered an excellent outline of the interplay between mind and heart, knowledge and virtue in evolving good values and arriving at a consensus.

Bernie identified the dynamics of external and internal elements in the forming of consensus.

Rene Azurin stressed the need for electoral and judicial reforms and the elimination of discretionary powers of government officials over the allocation of funds. Rene cited official discretion in the allocation and disbursement of funds as the root cause of corruption.
The discussion thus entered the realm of the chicken and egg conundrum: should it be values change or system change that must happen first?

Rene thinks that we must try to accomplish what can already be done and that system change eventually accelerates value reformation. I am of the thinking that system is a mere reflection of the values of a society and that unless the values change first, there is little or no hope for real system change.

The motor car was produced because society demanded a faster mode of transport — people wanted to junk the horse and carriage. Likewise, democracy evolves from a people who have realized the inequities of the old monarchy. There can be no democracy where there is no burning desire for a government for, by and of the people.

But more than just wanting democracy, people must also know and understand the reasons why the old system failed. People who love to be ruled by a monarch cannot want democracy bad enough to be willing to fight and die for it.

We were under martial law for 14 years because many Filipinos then thought that we were better off under a totalitarian regime.

In the Philippine context, we end up repeating our mistakes because too many false prophets have filled our people with the wrong information, the wrong analysis of the problem and the wrong solutions. Our people have been promised solutions to such immediate problems as education, employment and the like but they have not been led to understand the broader dynamics that create our major problems.

Most Filipinos are oblivious of the oligarchy, the monopoly of economic and political power and the absence of people empowerment. Many so-called educated Filipinos are not even aware of the real roots of our problems. We are so easily misled to adopting polices that are detrimental to us.

Embracing globalization and joining the Iraq War are two such examples. Take a look at what globalization did to our agriculture industry. We joined the Iraq War without realizing it was against our best interest which is to protect the Filipino overseas workers in the Middle East. We realized our folly only after a Filipino overseas worker — Angelo de la Cruz — was abducted and was about to be killed if our government didn't change its Iraq policy.

We were given our independence and democracy in 1946. We had to win it back in 1986 from Marcos. And yet we continue to suffer today from a failure of democracy.

Everyone Is Doing It?

Rene Azurin

A writer – I cannot now recall which one – reflecting on his society in the post-French Revolution era said, "In an absolutely corrupt age, the safest course is to do what others do." I have been thinking of this rather cynical but perceptive observation lately because it seems to describe what is going on in our own society today.

Both public officials and private individuals engage in corrupt practices – or at least close their eyes to these – because it now seems the safest thing to do. Whether such practices involve taking (providing) kickbacks for government contracts or accepting (paying) bribes to alter election returns, not going along with what everyone else is doing can be very dangerous not only to one's health but also to one's otherwise legitimate means of livelihood.

What is to me most significant about the latest SWS survey on corruption is that the respondents were 705 managers of Filipino firms drawn randomly from the rosters of participating business associations and federations. Were the survey's respondents made up of the public at large, the findings might reveal only perceptions of corruption, not real instances of it.

But, a survey of those who themselves would have personal knowledge of the bribery of high government officials – because they would invariably have had to authorize it – is a really telling indicator of the extent of corruption in our society today.

Notably, over half of the businessmen surveyed said that "most or all" firms gave bribes to win government contracts. The rest of the respondents may have thought that corruption was not so pervasive as to merit a "most or all" assessment or may have simply been psychologically predisposed to opt for the safer and more diplomatic judgment of "some".

In any case, the reported findings are a terrible indictment both of our public officials and the businessmen themselves, whether or not they do it because it is "the safest course".

Moreover, it is not just that people who are in a position to know say that corruption is rampant and reaches the highest levels of government. What the SWS survey also reports is that these people say that they do not believe that certain institutions of government crucial to eliminating corruption – like the House of Representatives (-32), the Department of Justice (-19), the Philippine National Police (-23), the Senate (-7), the Presidential Anti-Graft Commission (-8), and the Office of the President (-3) – are not at all sincere about dealing with this extremely serious problem.

The figures in parentheses are net negative ratings, revealing that a larger percentage of the respondents distrust those agencies than trust them, the number indicating the difference. That such important institutions in the fight against corruption are dismissed as insincere can be taken to mean that people have largely given up on this government, at least as far as corruption is concerned.

The ramifications of the survey are profound. On one level, it implies that most businessmen have accepted the fact that corruption in this government has no chance of being eliminated and must therefore just be tolerated as "the safest course". That rationalizes various forms of bribery, at all levels: either resort to it – "corruption is part of the way the government works" – or resign oneself to not getting what one wants from government, perhaps causing one's business to fail. On another level, it suggests that most people are already convinced that this government does not exist for their benefit but, rather, for the personal benefit of certain public officials who now hold high government positions. That rationalizes all sorts of things, some too potentially horrifying for someone committed to liberal democracy to even mention.

To be fair, such survey findings have been reported of previous governments and will very likely be reported of the next one. This shows that corruption is now so ingrained in our system that it may no longer be possible to eliminate. If one were feeling charitable, one might say that even the best efforts of honest and sincere individual officials who are placed in positions of importance in government cannot change the culture and practice of corruption.

If one were in a cynical mood, however, one would say that such positions of importance in government are sought precisely – and held on too aggressively – because of the great opportunities they offer for personal benefit and aggrandizement. This probably explains why the businessmen surveyed are so distrustful of the sincerity of the agencies of government supposed to actually fight corruption.

It also implies that we citizens better ditch any expectations that these government officials will actually work to reform the system in anything other than a cosmetic manner.

This is why a friend, *Philippine Star* columnist William Esposo, does not feel that trying to introduce reforms in the system offers any real chances of success. If (as the survey findings reveal) corruption is now so pervasive, this says a great deal about the sorry state of our nation's moral values. Billy argues, passionately, that unless these moral values are changed first, one cannot hope to change the practice of government. Thus, he feels that efforts of would-be reformers should be directed first at values change, not system change. Change the values, he says, and the system will follow.

If I do not buy completely Billy's argument, it is not because I do not subscribe to his premise but because I have difficulty conceiving of a practical way to go about changing society's values on such a large scale without first changing at least certain elements of the environment in which people operate.

As the experiments of behavioral psychologist B.F. Skinner have demonstrated, the design of the environment in which a subject operates is what dictates the subject's behavior. Make the appropriate changes in the environment, Skinner famously concluded, and you can change any behavior.

Accordingly, I continue to hope that there are still enough reforming elements in our society who might be persuaded to put their collective weight behind efforts to introduce some changes in the existing system, specifically in the structure of economic incentives.

Realizing that we need to pick only a few targets in order to focus efforts and thus boost the chances of success, my priority for such changes would be the immediate scrapping of the obscene economic incentives of public office (like the legislative and executive pork barrel and the extensive powers of government officials to regulate businesses) and the adoption of certain procedural and structural reforms in the justice system to improve law enforcement in this country.

Notwithstanding its generally discouraging revelations, there is something encouraging in the SWS survey. Two out of five of the managers surveyed reported that they are now spending for anti-fraud and anti-corruption initiatives in their companies. I hope that this correctly indicates that these managers have decided to depart from "the safest course" of doing what everyone is doing.

To Political Democracy thru Financial Democracy

Veredigno Atienza

On June 14 - June 16, 2007, the Liga ng mga Barangay ng Makati sponsored a small-business finance seminar at the Grand Villas (Bay, Laguna).

The main inspiration for the seminar was R. A. 9178, titled "Barangay Micro Business Enterprises Act of 2002". This law mandates the creation of a BMBE registration office under the Treasurer in every city and town in the Philippines. BMBE stands for "Barangay Micro-Business Enterprise".

BMBE's are defined by law to be enterprises with assets less than Philippine Peso 3,000,000, excluding the land. Such assets can be funded by loans or equity. The qualified lines of business are: a) the production and processing of goods, including agri processing, b) trading, and c) services, excluding services covered by government licensing exams.

The law offers incentives, such as exemption from the payment of income tax, and exemption from the payment of the minimum daily wage, except for employees already enjoying the minimum daily wage, as prescribed by law.

The law likewise requires the provision of credit by specific government financial institutions, and the provision of assistance in the areas of technology transfer, production and management training, and marketing by specified government agencies. Section Thirteen of the law provides civil and criminal penalties for the directors and officers of the specified agencies who unreasonably fail to provide for BMBE's as required by the BMBE law. To further emphasize the importance of the BMBE law, the BMBE exposures of accredited financial institutions can qualify as performance under the Agri-Agra Law, and the Magna Carta for Small and Medium-Scale Industries at twice the value of said exposures.

All in all, the BMBE law is the best chance so far of the Filipino micro entrepreneur to push his business forward. Assuming it will be sufficiently implemented, the BMBE law stands out as a unique and concrete government effort to help the entrepreneur, perhaps more tangible than praiseworthy exhortations to have "sipag at tiyaga" and to "go negosyo."

And yet there is something troubling if not sinister about the BMBE law. The law has to provide a "special credit window". Why does it have to be a special window? Because micro-enterprises need micro finance, countryside lending programs and special credit windows. Otherwise they will not be attended to, because the dominant financial market forces find micros unbankable and low-priority.

In his overview of the national credit delivery system, Milton Abanto, vice-president of Small Business Finance and Guarantee Corporation, presented a staircase where the unbankables start at the lowest rung, working their way up to higher levels of creditworthiness and bankability, and into the arms of larger, better-funded, more established, and more sophisticated financial institutions. It will take the unbankables a lifetime and perhaps even never to attain the higher levels of bankability. Such is the fate of 99.6% of Philippine enterprises, since 99.6% of our enterprises are micro, small, and medium. There must be a shorter and surer way of achieving bankability.

A shorter way of attaining bankability for most Filipinos is possible if the Philippines will have financial democracy. More ordinary businessmen will become more bankable if the supply and scale of financial institutions that will consider them bankable will increase. More ordinary Filipinos will become bankable entrepreneurs if the institutional infrastructure in support of their entrepreneurship will attain a meaningful scale. There is no shortage of ordinary people who want to and can be independent businessmen. The problem is not in the demand for funds, but in the supply of funds and opportunities.

Financial democracy refers to ordinary people having a larger share and control of banking and financial assets. Financial democracy involves a wider and easier access of the ordinary people to financial assets. Financial democracy happens when a large enough proportion of banking and financial institutions, especially universal banks, becomes subject to the ownership and control of the ordinary people.

Furthermore, a shorter way to bankability depends on the country's awakening: that there can be no true political democracy unless there is first economic democracy and that there can be no economic democracy unless there is first financial democracy.

The single largest obstacle to having a fully functioning Philippine political democracy where the needs of the majority are properly addressed as a result of suffrage is the high concentration of economic assets in the hands of a few families. In turn the high economic concentration of assets can be traced to the high concentration of financial and banking assets in a few families, and vice-versa. Most Filipinos are outside the economic and financial loop, within which information is more reliable and abundant, opportunities are larger and more attainable, and within which connections are more useful and profitable.

Before proceeding further, I must first add a caveat; the above discussion does not insinuate anything of the following sort: 1) that big business is per se bad, or 2) that the people should bring the rich down, line them up against the wall, and distribute the wealth of the rich among the poor. Regarding the first point, big business is not per se bad. On the contrary, we need scale in many industries to be world-competitive. But scale should not be at the expense of a fair economic structure. As for the second point, this is nonsense and will be a bloody mess. Not even taxing the rich to death will enrich the poor. Rather, we must find more effective and efficient ways and means to bring the less fortunate, less advantaged, and less capable up to higher levels of capacity, opportunity and privilege.

What vehicle is required to help attain financial democracy while serving as a laboratory and training ground for the attainment of political democracy? What mechanism can provide extensive practice in intelligent discussion, weighing of options with financial implications, and the application of policies and guidelines, which are necessary for the functioning of a financial democracy as well as a political democracy? What vehicle will provide lessons in the value and practice of the rule of law, of fair play, and of a broader and longer-term view? What vehicle will give training in giving greater weight to broader interests rather than to vested or funny-company interests?

Do these vehicles exist, or should it or they be designed? What are the other considerations? The vehicle should involve a real personal stake of the members, the measurement of performance, the transparency of measures of performance, the rewarding of good performance, the punishment of bad performance, and an understanding of the price, cost and value of good governance. It goes without saying that the vehicle should have peaceful and civil means of conflict resolution and management succession.

A people's universal bank could be that vehicle for the attainment of financial democracy and for the honing of skills necessary in making a political democracy functional. A universal bank of the people, by the people and for the people. A corporate body with a reasonably egalitarian outlook. One investor, one vote in choosing the Board of Directors and in deciding on key issues presented to the stockholders at large. Every investor, equal value. Each investor basically an ordinary Filipino, unaligned with any conglomerate or political group or government body.

Each investor an investprosumer, or one who invests in a company that produces the products and services that he himself avails of as a consumer. Each investor presently with negligible powers, but has the power to choose. Investment in a people's universal bank can hone the ordinary Filipino's power to choose, such as –

directors, bank initiatives, basic product lines, and other items in the long menu necessary for making a universal bank work.

For our people, a people's universal bank is a more manageable territory compared to strengthening the weak Philippine state, and to reforming government agencies or Congress or the military or the police or the judicial system or the electoral system or the tax regime or the general competitiveness of Philippine industries or the competition policies of various sectors held hostage by monopolists and oligopolists.

What businesses should the PUB get into? Nothing fancy, nothing unproven. No funding of mergers and acquisitions, no complicated project finance. Only plain vanilla businesses like: housing loans, car and vehicle loans, credit cards, student loans, salary loans, microfinance, life insurance, fire and auto insurance, pensions. Not that these businesses have no risks, but the right management and personnel can take care of those risks.

And since the universal banks and conglomerates of the tycoons capture allied and adjunct businesses, why should a people's universal bank not capture the businesses that serve the people's foremost needs? Why should the ordinary people and the poor people always have to pay more for less, while the well-endowed have the facility to pay less for more of units purchased? Of course the answer is the theory of price or the law of supply and demand, of which economies of scale is a vital principle. But then again, should not the greater mass of people make the same law work for them, since they themselves provide the numbers, the mass, and the scale?

Whatever social capital there is should be harnessed to produce financial capital, which will in turn have the potential to become political capital. Financial democracy is an excellent foundation for political democracy, not the other way around. A democracy founded on financial elitism can only be an elite democracy, which basically caters to the needs of the elite or elites, while paying lip service to the needs of the masses. In such elite democracy, the masses and the ordinary folk are outside the political-economic loop, getting crumbs during an economic boom and getting displaced during a bust.

In thinking about financial democracy, there are two temptations we must be careful of: first, that financial democracy is a futile objective because in any society some people are simply and truly just smarter and faster, or second, that financial democracy is unnecessary due to the plethora of mechanisms already available to alleviate the condition of the poor.

A recent work seems to confirm the first line of thinking as far as Southeast Asia is concerned. Read Joe Studwell's "Asian Godfathers: Money and Power in Hongkong and Southeast Asia". Also read Asian Development Bank's Key Indicators 2007 report.

As for the second line of thinking, media chic gives the impression and reinforces the belief that charity, disaster relief, philanthropy, corporate social responsibility, patronage, microfinance, business, and suffrage are more than enough to help the lower-income classes.

Unfortunately, the above mechanisms have limits, some more restrictive than others. Charity feeds people for a day or even longer, but not for a lifetime. Patronage goes a longer way, but depends on what the patron needs from his constituents. Disaster relief ends where the business of rebuilding lives and properties begins. Philanthropy and CSR are spurious and even hypocritical when the philanthropists engage in illegal, corrupt, unfair, predatory, unethical, wasteful, and/or unproductive business practices. Where philanthropy is just another form of marketing and advertising, it is self-serving, and vulnerable to being replaced by a more cost-efficient component of the marketing mix.

Microfinance, subcontracting and other business solutions for the poor hold great promise. Housing for the poor, export opportunities for the poor, land for the poor, phone cards for the poor, and other business initiatives are all laudable. However, Herman B. Leonard wrote this caveat in his article "When Is Doing Business with the Poor Good – for the Poor?": "Part of the challenge of socially valuable entrepreneurship focused on the base of the pyramid is to design products and ventures in a way that serves the larger social interests of the people fueling the transaction, rather than simply finding ways to create, capture, and then drain value from low-income communities."

Suffrage has its limits too. Where votes are bought and sold like commodities, suffrage loses its value and power in effecting change for the betterment of the people. The main victim of prostituted suffrage is any and all hope for better government governance. Votes are exchanged for a day's meal in places where most of the people have a negligible share of economic assets, regardless whether these are financial or non-financial assets. As we have been trying to say all along, political democracy is not possible where there is no economic and financial democracy.

Programs in education, health, and infrastructure depend on the resources generated via suffrage, governance, even business and philanthropy. While education has made possible the manpower exports and business process outsourcing that sustain the economy, education has many inadequacies. Health resources are in turn not coping with population growth and the migration of medical and allied-medical professionals. Infrastructure efforts are bedeviled by funding problems. Lastly, education, health and infrastructure are lucrative feeding grounds for grafters and corruptors, who grow rich and fat, as in other places, with impunity and without remorse, at the expense of the poor and everybody else.

By a process of elimination, we have to come to terms with the need for financial democracy. It is a necessary complement to the other poverty- alleviating mechanisms. It is a challenging goal that offers more prospects of failure than success, and yet it is a goal that simply has to be targeted, lest we wither in despair.

Small-time finance, such as microfinance, salary loans, and BMBE financing are mere tokens if we visualize financial democracy as it should and can be. The Filipino people should target having a real financial democracy, not its mere shadow or caricature. Small-time finance is a palliative, a token, a shadow, that will just perpetuate the position of the ordinary Filipino outside the loop, in his own homeland, in his own country. Para kang pumapasok sa sarili mong bahay sa likod hindi sa harapan, at nakikiraan ka pa.

So how do we get from here to there? It is highly possible that what brought us here won't get us there. Talk is cheap, so cheap.

Fortunately, so is faith. If ten million ordinary Filipinos were to contribute ten thousand pesos as equity or 'taya' (bet) in a people's universal bank, then we will get there. Then we will have a universal bank with a capitalization of one hundred billion pesos, with a scale that can make a national difference. Indeed, faith empowers, a story repeated many times in human history.

The solution to poverty and many ills related to poverty is at hand. The solution is so simple. Thru the faith of the ordinary Filipino in his fellow ordinary Filipino, thru his faith in himself, thru his faith in Divine Inspiration, the people's universal bank is within reach. Alone the ordinary Filipino is powerless; with many other Filipinos, he is powerful. To break the shackles and cycle of poverty does the ordinary Filipino have any other choice but to trust one another?

If eleven million Filipinos were able to make a senator out of a young, brash, talented but inexperienced naval officer with a limited campaign budget and presently under detention for charges involving coup d'etat; if jobless Filipinos can shell out PHP 200,000 for an overseas job that may not even exist; a people's universal bank managed by independent and unaligned Filipino banking professionals is totally within reach.

This universal bank will make the ordinary Filipino more bankable in a quicker and more likely manner. More important, this universal bank will be our people's great experiment in financial democracy and eventually political democracy. If they can make their own universal bank succeed, they can one day find the means and will to make our Philippine democracy succeed. Tiyak yon.

The necessary progression from social capital to financial capital to financial democracy to economic democracy to political capital to political democracy may seem like a play on words, but it is grounded in history and reality and will entail a lot of work, sacrifice, pain, trust and faith. The alternative may be unthinkable.

Index of Contributors

Reviews

218

www.ingramcontent.com/pod-product-compliance
Lightning Source LLC
Chambersburg PA
CBHW031955190326
41520CB00007B/260